More Praise

"Evolution and growth is always
book provides practical advice on   ... the
midst of change."

−*Kurt Tunnell*
Managing Partner, Bricker & Eckler

"Throughout my career, I've managed the unexpected. *Go With It*
gives anyone great ideas to improvise and be effective."

−*Dan Creekmur*
President, Columbia Gas of Ohio, a NiSource Company

"The speed of innovation is reliant on the people who drive change.
This book allows any team to up their game, collaborate radically,
and improvise. That means faster to market with better outcomes!"

−*Ben Verwer*
Vice President, Strategic Initiatives, BD Diagnostics

"Real life is all improv! *Go With It* outlines usable skills that allow
professionals to engage in behaviors that increase success, and get
us all comfortable with discomfort."

−*LaChandra Baker*
President, Columbus Chapter, International Association of
Business Communicators

"This practical little book offers fresh and powerful insights into
how anyone can learn to make themselves more creative and to
help others by leading them to much more creative and superior
outcomes. I thoroughly enjoyed reading it!"

−*Alan Robinson*
Co-Author, Ideas Are Free *and* Corporate Creativity

GO

WITH

IT

Embrace the
Unexpected to
Drive Change

KAREN HOUGH

atd
PRESS

ATD Press is an internationally renowned source of insightful and practical information on
talent development, training, and professional development.

ATD Press
1640 King Street
Alexandria, VA 22314 USA

Ordering information: Books published by ATD Press can be purchased by visiting ATD's
website at www.td.org/books or by calling 800.628.2783 or 703.683.8100.

Library of Congress Control Number: 2017935217

ISBN-10: 1-56286-571- 4
ISBN-13: 978-1-56286-571-9
e-ISBN: 978-1-56286-574-0

ATD Press Editorial Staff
Director: Kristine Luecker
Manager: Christian Green
Community of Practice Manager, Human Capital: Ann Parker
Developmental Editor: Kathryn Stafford
Senior Associate Editor: Melissa Jones
Text Design: Iris Sanchez
Cover Design: Faceout Studio, Derek Thornton
Illustrator: Francelyn Fernandez

Printed by Versa Press Inc., East Peoria, IL

To all the people who were ever slapped upside the head, caught unawares, tripped up, or blew it. And instead of crying or hiding, they got up, started over, learned something new, or laughed. You are my people. We're the ones who never get to learn lessons the easy way. And that's a good thing. That means we're improvisers.

Contents

Preface

Improvisation is the bedrock of my life. It affects how I behave, work, parent, communicate, and create. It wove itself into my DNA because the moment I learned about improv, I realized that anything was possible. And my serendipitous life path is a reflection of that improviser's belief in every possibility.

I've lived several lives, and all of them have been in the midst of innovators. Whether I was creating theater in the moment on the improvisational stage, working on the front lines of the Internet revolution, or developing scientists and engineers as a consultant, I've had the good fortune to watch innovation happening. And what struck me, over those decades of observation and participation, was that innovators behave in special ways. When I was immersed in teams of innovators, I admired their utterly natural ability to deal with dichotomy, prepare, play, and think upside down. However, when I would move to a group or corporation bound up in old patterns of thought and action that quality vanished; I found the difference alarming.

The good news is that even those groups who were not working well together could learn. They could grow, develop, and change their patterns of behavior to be more creative and innovative—and those changes came from embracing improvisational techniques. I've worked with pharmaceutical scientists who wanted to accelerate their fuzzy front-end work on new drugs, technologists who needed to get their breakthrough idea to market, and executives who had to get their teams working and innovating together. This book is the outcome of those many experiences across myriad industries and teams.

My company, ImprovEdge, has created training and development for Fortune 1000 employees and executives since 1998 using the principles of improvisation, paired with research in psychology, human behavior, and neuroscience. Corporate leaders and teams have applied those practices to great success, becoming more flexible, creative, and innovative.

I first learned to improvise as an undergraduate at Yale. Soon after, I trained with the Second City of Chicago, performed and started my own troupes, and had a wonderful acting career in TV, film, radio, and the stage. I zigzagged at one point, taking eight years to stretch and challenge myself by working in the network engineering industry. I'm not kidding! Yes, a liberal arts–educated actor can go to work in IT. (And if I can do that, then I'm sure you can improvise.) I helped startups go public or be acquired, and although I was taking tech classes and cramming every night, I continued improvising during the day. Those techniques allowed me to be flexible, creative, collaborative, and more successful than I ever imagined possible.

These incredible experiences also led me to create content–from narratives of what is possible, of what works best. The Yes! Deck is a toolkit I developed comprising 29 cards full of tips, ideas, and exercises for trainers and managers (you'll see examples of these exercises at the end of many of the chapters in this book). I also wrote two books, *The Improvisation Edge: Secrets to Building Trust and Radical Collaboration at Work* and *Be the Best Bad Presenter Ever: Break the Rules, Make Mistakes and Win Them Over*, which is an award-winning book published in four languages. Those books allowed me to dive deeply into team dynamics and personal development. They've inspired thousands of people to behave differently, take risks, and throw out old conventions to emerge as more effective individuals and teams. And that theme kept driving me to wonder, "What's the next, most important application of this work?"

We must innovate. And I believe that the behaviors of improvisation can directly drive our ability to continue to evolve and improve. There are such pressing issues of global technology, science, health, and welfare at stake as we fly into the 21st century–and with everything moving so quickly, we have to approach this with flexibility, humor, and focus. We need to innovate as improvisers.

This book on innovation came about through my relationship with ATD, which has hosted many of my presentations on innovation and improvisation at conferences and encouraged me to share my blog posts and webcasts with its members. That excitement led to this book, in which I intend to inspire you to engage in improvisational behaviors to drive innovation in your life and work.

So where does innovation come from? The front lines—the everyday interactions that create small "Eureka!" moments. But many companies and individuals struggle with managing those early ideas. For example, my company once worked with an insurance client that realized great ideas from its call centers weren't bubbling up. Many of those front-line professionals had unusual ideas about how to serve customers better and more quickly. Unfortunately, whenever they tried to introduce those ideas, they received negative responses from their managers: "We're too busy right now." "No, we have to follow the scripts and protocol." Or worst, "That's above your pay grade—could you get back to work?"

The alarm bell for this company really went off when one frustrated employee took her idea to a competitor. It saved the competitor between two and 10 cents per call, which over thousands of calls is a significant savings. The idea had been formed in my client's call center, but because the employee received no support and didn't feel valued or like a real member of the team, she left, taking her innovative idea with her.

If her manager had only improvised a bit when she introduced the idea, that story might have ended differently. The innovation could have stayed in house. And more important, a valuable member of the team could still be working there.

There are many methods being touted out there to drive innovation, so what does improv bring to the table? By changing the way we interact with our teams, so that we wrap in the simple rules and behaviors that come from the improvisational stage, we can effect incredible change and innovation in our work and lives. Innovation comes from positivity, acceptance, a willingness to take risks, and the courage to apply creative ideas. Those obvious behaviors that affect corporate innovation are the same that apply to improvisation.

We are all improvisers. Although we may believe that we are set in our ways and don't handle change well, we actually all have to improvise every day. With this book, you will not only understand how improvisation works, but also be able to use its techniques, secrets, and behaviors to be more innovative in your own life and work.

Introduction

Innovation is a learned behavior. And improvisation is your guide.

Improvisers arrive onstage without a script with the goal of creating entire one-act plays on the fly. It sounds terrifying to some people, yet improv has clear guidelines that allow troupes to be collaborative and innovative in the moment.

The reason an improv troupe can create scenes out of thin air is because of the foundational principle "Yes, and." No matter what I contribute on stage, my troupe immediately does two things: agrees with me (yes) and adds to my idea (and).

So if I declare, "I'm a Warrior Queen!" a fellow improviser may say, "Yes, you are my Warrior Queen, and I'm your shield bearer!" and so the scene is off. You see, the *yes* is the acknowledgment that we agree and we're here to play. The *and* is the building block. We can't just simply agree, then hang our scene partner out to dry by making him come up with all the ideas. We have to say and to add to it—increase the possibility, get onboard, spice it up, move forward.

There's a real magic to those two simple words, and they are surprisingly revolutionary to some corporate cultures. Our natural inclination is to say no to new ideas. We're actually wired for it, and our immediate skepticism acts as a sort of defense mechanism. Researchers have found that in multiple cultures and languages, 50 percent of our emotion words are negative, while 30 percent are positive and 20 percent are neutral (ABC News 2005). Our overuse of negative words also affects our communication and relationships, making it difficult to build trust and work together effectively. And negativity is anathema to improvisation.

On the improv stage, it's called denial and it kills good improv. My favorite example is the apple scene, which we use during training workshops with our corporate clients. This simple scene shows corporate audiences what can happen if you deny everything onstage. Here's how it works: I ask a volunteer to join me onstage. The person is usually excited, very nervous to be in front of her colleagues, and very brave, as she is usually the first volunteer. I instruct her to improvise with me by opening up the scene with the simple line, "Here, I brought you an apple!" However, instead of playing along, I immediately deny: "That's not an apple."

I'm always impressed by how creative and tenacious my volunteers can be–they describe the apple, insist that it's a gift, try to get me to smell or taste it, and yet I just keep saying, "No. It's not. No."

Sometimes after so much denial, the volunteer will finally say, "What do YOU think it is?!" She is clearly frustrated and doesn't know what to say next. The audience, while pulling for her and starting to hate me, is confused and getting bored because nothing is happening in the scene.

After I end the scene, we discuss what happened: How did it feel to hear no so much? What was your response when you just kept getting shot down? Answers range from frustration to anger to retreat. I have a sad memory of one man actually admitting, "This is what it felt like my first week on the job. I haven't contributed an idea since. I just do what I'm told because who wants to feel stupid or unvalued every time they try to contribute?" Yikes.

And that's the rub. Negativity is a serious problem for innovation, and words are powerful. Once most people hear no, they are statistically less likely to contribute again.

I've had people monitor their language use and report on the number of negative versus positive words they use. They're often surprised by what they discover. I had one shocked general counsel sit down with me after only half a day and say, "I need some coaching here. I've been frustrated by the lack on involvement on my team for two years, and I just realized I haven't said a positive sentence all morning."

The key, too, is that we may not understand how little it takes to lose a team member. Again and again, we hear corporate participants report that it only takes a few instances of *no* for them to cease contributing.

Meanwhile, back to my improv partner onstage. I apologize for my negativity and promise to be a better improviser. This time, when she offers me an apple, I respond with something like, "Yes! It's a gorgeous apple and I bet you picked it in your grandmother's orchard!"

It's incredible where they go from there. Volunteers who have never improvised before start adding onto the scene and it takes off in the most humorous, unexpected, and creative ways. I had one scene partner (who had never improvised before) get the entire audience to sing an apple pie song and pretend to pick apples off of an imaginary orchard over their heads!

This "yes, and" behavior is critical to innovative teams because it allows all ideas to be contributed. And it allows people to feel heard. Even if a contribution isn't used in the end, the process of listening, agreeing to hear them, and discussing an idea is monumentally affirming.

The key to "yes, and" is that it encourages contribution. Some managers are afraid it means they have to accept anything their team says. On the contrary, "yes, and" is about saying, "Yes, I hear you. And let's discuss this idea and please continue to contribute."

Many scenes on the improv stage are dumped if they end up not being funny or working, but at least we tried them out. The same thing happens in corporate teams. An environment of acceptance, discussion, and addition allows ideas to be vetted, rather than trashed before even being tried.

This improvisational behavior is key to creating innovative environments and teams. How we choose to behave can either foster innovation or shut it down. There are also a lot of stereotypes and misconceptions about innovation that are getting in our way. We think innovation is reliant upon huge undertakings, gigantic creative efforts, and blinding feats of change—it's got to be big, expensive, and world-changing. We believe we have to be Renaissance people who seamlessly write symphonies while penning novels and programming groundbreaking smartphone applications.

That's a lot of pressure and we need to get over it. We need to realize that we all have the capability to innovate. And the behaviors we need can be learned. By anyone.

Many meaningful innovations are actually a series of small steps that come from ordinary people working together in extraordinary ways. When a call center pro figures out how to fix a customer's problem in one minute rather than three, or a group of managers sees a way to improve a product and save a nickel in every transaction—that's innovation. And those little eureka moments add up to big advantages for organizations.

But how do we make sure those small, good ideas bubble up? How do individuals become more innovative and how can managers and leaders engage their teams to tease out the solutions that may be hiding in plain sight? It all has to do with how we interact, how we choose to collaborate and communicate, and whether we are willing to play.

How we choose to behave has much more influence on innovative outcomes than a million strategic initiatives; that is because strategic initiatives only happen, and only work, when every person is working to drive that strategy. The little things we do every day at our desk or in our home are the tiny wheels that push big changes forward.

Behavior drives innovation. So how do we learn to think and behave differently? What model for behavioral innovation exists that can guide this change? Get ready—the answer is:

Improvisation!

I know, the exclamation mark worries you. Just hang in there—this is exciting news! The behaviors improvisers use in every performance to create shows out of nothing are the same behaviors that great innovators put to use. Our choices about how we interact, live, question, play, and think are the building blocks to every innovation we could ever hope for—and a very simple way to approach very big problems.

We all have the ability to engage in behaviors that can change the way we work, live, think, and innovate. And yes, your brain can be trained to think more creatively and you can engage in behaviors that will allow you to innovate. And the same is true for your colleagues and family and friends. We tend to believe that creative ability is something we are born with, or not; that in the nature versus nurture argument, we come up short if we aren't born to a creative family. Yet, when researchers studied more than 110 pairs of identical and fraternal twins they found that only about 30 percent of creative ability is attributable to genetics. This means nurture is responsible for more than two-thirds of a person's ability to solve problems and be creative, innovative, and playful. In other words, if people want to be more creative, they can engage in behaviors to boost their creativity, especially if they grow up around other people who behave collaboratively (Reznikoff et al. 1973).

Carol Dweck (2006), in her brilliant narrative *Mindset: The New Psychology of Success*, discusses people's ability to change how they think and behave. She even admits that she had to undergo a significant change in mindset and behavior after she earned her PhD. It took intentional work; she was not only capable, it set the path for her life's work. Change isn't always easy, but the human capacity for growth throughout life is extraordinary.

In three independent studies tracking creativity training by the University of Oklahoma, the University of Georgia, and Taiwan's National Chengchi University, researchers found that the effects of improvisationally based creativity training radically improved subjects' abilities to think, reason, and create novel solutions. By integrating the processes of improvisation, subjects taught themselves to use divergent thinking to come up with many ideas, and then use convergent thinking to combine all those ideas for novel results (Bronson and Merryman 2010).

I was having a rowdy conversation with my family one night, asking for their opinions about innovators. What makes an innovative person? My 11-year-old son, Trey, who had been quiet up to this point, suddenly answered, "They innovate themselves, Mom." His comment was so unexpected, the entire family stopped and considered. And I realized he nailed it. Almost every account of innovation and innovators that I had been gathering was about the person's ability to become—to improvise in the face of uncertainty or difficulty and write his own score. Just like a jazz musician, he created a new type of music that had never been heard before.

Lisa Seacat DeLuca changed from a frustrated outsider at college to IBM's most prolific inventor with more than 420 patents. Bessie Coleman, born to sharecroppers in 1892, went from impoverished girl to the first Native American–African American woman to earn a pilot's license. Hedy

Lamarr (yes, that Hedy Lamarr) may have been a femme fatale in movies, but she was bored offscreen and wanted to contribute to the World War II effort. So she tinkered around with machines and finally patented a technology that laid the groundwork for Wi-Fi and Bluetooth. Steve Jobs created technology that didn't sell; then he tried and failed again and again before he finally got to the world's most recognized technology, Apple computers (Jacobs 2015; Singh 2016; Griggs and Grinberg 2015).

They all went through years of learning, tinkering, failure, and effort to become the innovators they are and were. That is exactly how improvisers behave—they are constantly stretching, trying, failing, succeeding, and starting over. DeLuca, Coleman, Lamarr, and Jobs all innovated themselves. So can you.

About This Book

Go With It: Embrace the Unexpected to Drive Change will show you the methods, mindsets, and behaviors that drive improvisers. These techniques can be learned and nurtured, which in turn will nurture your ability to be an innovative person. And then you can model and teach those behaviors to others.

The first four chapters explore four major improvisational concepts that lead to behavioral innovation and change: embracing the unexpected, preparing like an improviser, playing in the moment, and thinking upside down. Each category is critical to putting on a good improv show—and critical to driving innovative behaviors. Then, the final chapter discusses how you can shape the future by managing change through improvisation. Additionally, each chapter features a case study based on real-life examples, an exercise for you to try with your team, and an improvisational sketch presenting Improvisation and Innovation as human characters.

Go With It is about changing, embracing the unexpected, and innovating—like an improviser. This cycle of growth is lifelong, and will allow you to be flexible, adaptable, and innovative, no matter what comes your way. This book will introduce you to the cycle that improvisers live in (Figure I-1):

- **Prepare.** We're constantly practicing, preparing, and setting the foundation. You never know when you'll need to perform.

- **Play.** We engage in play, exploration, and experimentation. Play tests the limits of our preparation so we can learn where we hit the mark and where we need more work.
- **Think.** We have to look at things upside down, in weird ways, and with diverse groups. We're always pushing the boundaries of our play and preparation.
- **Change.** When all that up-front work pays off, we have to embrace the change we discover. We have to evolve. And once those new skills are mastered, it's time to start again.

So enjoy! Everybody improvises. Even you.

Figure I-1. The Improv Cycle

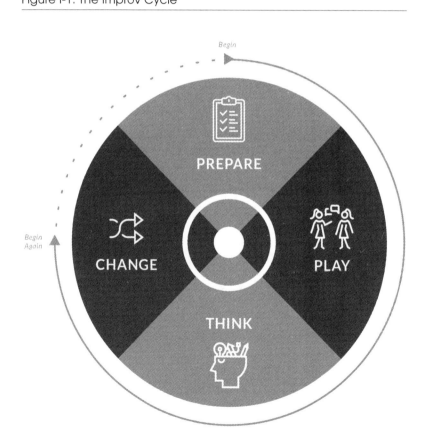

1

Embracing the Unexpected

A man goes down on his knee onstage and proposes to a woman. We (the audience) expect her to be thrilled and say, "Yes!" And although the actress may do that, it's far more interesting if she adds a look of shock, glances behind her back furtively, and seems to be accepting under duress. That creates tension. We wonder what is wrong, and why she seems so worried when the man is obviously happy. Now the troupe has a huge amount of room to play with, explore the scene, and try to uncover dramatic improv gold.

On the improvisational stage, if everything is wonderful and perfect all the time, the audience will get bored. We may accept everything as improvisers, but we also know that good theater comes out of dramatic conflict and character tension. While the acceptance and openness of "yes, and!" is critical to improvisation and innovation, things don't always go smoothly and much of the best improv and innovation grow out of surprise, problems that must be overcome, and tension.

Improvisers like to explore the uncomfortable and the unsaid. Comedy often arises from saying things no one else will say or exploring interactions that we all have but choose to ignore or avoid. Discomfort is an excellent marker of good improv and good innovation. It means you're leaning into the tension of the unknown. That takes courage.

Every night, improvisers get up onstage willing to meet the unexpected every moment of the show. We literally do not know what's going to happen from one moment to the next. And it's not always good—there are a lot of "off" nights in improv.

One misconception about improvisation is that we can hide problems from the audience. If something goes wrong, people assume we'll be able to cover and no one will be the wiser because we can improvise anything. Wrong! When a scene is out of sync, a character is called by the wrong name, or if two people are doing different things at the same time, everybody knows—the troupe, the audience, the sound and light pros up in the booth, sometimes even the ticket taker in the hallway.

That being said, some of the best and funniest moments in improv happen when things go horribly awry on stage. They are funny because the improvisers acknowledge that everything has gone off the tracks. Audiences love the moment when the performers realize their mistake, give each other a look or almost crack up, and figure out where to go from there. They might make wild, hysterical explanations or launch into utterly new story lines based on the surprise. In fact, some of the best shows I've done came out of a moment of uncertainty.

The "oops" is the obvious moment when anyone realizes something is off-kilter. How we choose to respond and act determine whether that oops remalns awful or has the potential to become a eureka. In improv, we are bound by our guidelines to acknowledge the issue to the audience, use it in the scene, and keep the show going. In fact, if we act as though nothing unusual occurred, the audience gets disappointed because they know something was weird. When we share the oops and bring the audience into the moment of discomfort, the entire theater becomes one team. Everybody is in on the joke! We can all enjoy the funny discomfort, and lean in and pull for the performers while they figure it out.

It takes courage to acknowledge a mistake. You may feel stupid, wonder if you'll get into trouble, or try to blame someone else. One of the unfortunate legacies of risk-averse, hierarchical organizations is that people are afraid to speak up, try something new, or make a mistake. Yet innovation and change come out of experimentation. It comes out of failure, learning from mistakes, and realizing that your new knowledge has led to a eureka.

Michael Jordan's meme on failure states, "I've missed more than 9,000 shots in my career. I've lost 300 games. Twenty-six times, I've been trusted to take the game-winning shot, and missed. I've failed over and over and over again in my life. And that is why I succeed."

Welcoming Diversity

Are all these surprises and issues easy? No! Tension, problems, and the unexpected are scary, even for improvisers. One of the most obvious ways to avoid tension is through lack of diversity. Diverse groups can be uncomfortable, but we undermine our ability to be innovative when we lean toward comfort and familiarity.

Many industries struggle with a lack of diversity in their ranks. Theatrical improvisation is no exception. Comedy has been stocked with funny white dudes for decades, which may have seemed fine for a while (and no knocks, they are really funny!), but it left no room for innovation. As a matter of fact, back when I was improvising in Chicago, major improv theaters capped their troupes at two women only. A director once looked at me in confusion when I questioned the practice and replied, "How many wives and girlfriends do we need on one stage?" My blood still boils to think about it. He could only envision me playing a female foil to the stars of the show—the men. The irony was how hard he laughed whenever I played against type, insisting on being the CEO or the gross, belching football fan in the scene. Comedy came from surprise—from changing up the obvious choice, which I loved doing with my troupe members.

So I set out to find and create troupes that had a wider range of people and ideas. It's not so much that I was angry. The comedy coming out at the time was fabulous. But there were so many opinions, ideas, and perspectives that weren't being explored, leaving a lot of potential untapped. I knew that at some point following the same formula would become boring for audiences.

Fortunately the comedy genre is evolving. Some of today's most impressive new material is coming from diverse comedians who are making us reconsider assumptions about race, gender, sexual orientation, and religion. They are bringing new formats, plot lines, characters, and perspectives to the psyche of the audience; it's untapped, risky, and above all, funny.

The research is in. Racially diverse teams outperform nondiverse teams by up to 35 percent (Hunt et al. 2015). And the employment website Glassdoor reports that almost 60 percent of employees wish their work environment was more diverse. Diversity is also important for workplace culture. When companies promote and train for inclusion, they solve problems faster and more creatively, which is reflected in their revenue. Teams where men and women feel equal earn more than 40 percent more revenue, and bilingual employees earn 10 percent more than single language employees no matter what the language (Badal 2014; White 2014).

A lack of diversity may help you achieve results on a standardized, simple operation, because the comfort, familiarity, and sameness of more homogeneous teams keep outcomes consistent. Diversity, on the other hand, breeds innovation. To innovate is often uncomfortable; it makes you question what you thought you knew, and introduces divergent concepts. It's not always fun, but improvisation and innovation are about challenge and pushing outside preconceived boundaries.

To be more innovative, resist your ingrained survival instincts, which you've honed through years of being right, avoiding risk, working with people just like you, and wanting to feel safe. Move toward the new behaviors slowly if you need to; try failing in a safe environment first. Learn something new and engage in the frustration of being a beginner before you put your job on the line at work.

This is tension, in all its glory. An individual, team, or organization's ability to integrate innovative behaviors and thinking may at first seem like an elusive goal. But it's critical that we explore the interplay of improvisational and innovative behaviors. There is enormous tension in the process of going from a creative idea to innovation.

Tension as a Driver

Creativity is the ability to envision anything and see the impossible working; innovation is the application of creativity. In its empirical form, creativity is basically the theory, idea, and vision—it must be applied. The moment that you paint on a canvas, write notes on a score, or design a building, creativity is transformed into innovation. That's what changes everything—that's innovation.

Simply put: **Creativity + Application = Innovation.**

Creativity:

The ability to transcend traditional ideas, rules, patterns, relationships, or the like, and create meaningful new ideas, forms, methods, and interpretations. Also known as originality, progressiveness, or imagination.

E. Paul Torrance, an American educational psychologist, is well known for his research on creativity. He challenged the importance of IQ tests as the single indicator of intelligence, believing in the importance of creative thinking skills, which can be increased through practice. Torrance defined creativity as the ability to alternate between divergent and convergent thinking. In divergent thinking, we come up with many ideas and see unusual connections and endless possibility. In convergent thinking, seemingly unrelated things suddenly connect, allowing us to envision brand-new solutions.

In 1958, Torrance performed a series of creativity tests on more than 400 Minneapolis children, and then tracked them over their lifetimes. He found that the children who continued to think and behave creatively won patents, founded businesses, performed in artistic and corporate leadership, won awards, designed buildings, and wrote books, music, and public policy. They were creative improvisers, yet they also achieved through innovation. They accessed both sides of the behavioral coin: the ability to come up with interesting and novel ideas as improvisers and the tenacity to do something about them as innovators.

Like any good coin analogy, creativity and improvisation versus innovation and execution offer two very different sides. (And the discussion around which is heads and which is tails will be held after hours.) They rely upon each other and are symbiotic in many ways. They are also highly different, and often clash in the corporate environment.

We must allow room and space for creativity and improvisation, which entails positivity, "yes, and," oops to eureka!, openness, and craziness. However, once we start to execute on those ideas, we desperately need the organization, detail-orientation, and drive of a project manager crossed with a financial editor. There's inherent tension there—let the rule-followers in too soon, and ideas are squashed. Leave the execution to the dreamers and nothing will ever get done.

Vijay Govindarajan, of the Harvard Business School and Dartmouth's Tuck School of Business, researched the intrinsic issue in innovation and found that it is not that organizations lack creativity; rather, they:

- don't go bold enough on their ideas—they shut down the dreamers and the crazy talk way too soon
- cannot execute—they become overwhelmed or cannot figure out how to bring ideas to life.

So how do we bridge that gap? How do we address the behaviors necessary for both sides of that behavioral coin? We must encourage creative people to speak up and build good ideas, while simultaneously giving everyone the resilience and courage to hang on through a difficult execution. From a behavioral standpoint, we must not only be champions of both styles, but protectors of very different processes.

One of Govindarajan's most compelling examples of that tension is from his research on reverse-innovation, a term he coined with his colleague, Chris Trimble. In developed countries, we tend to see innovation as new, high-end, and technological. We assume that greater levels of wealth and education lead to better innovation, so we rarely look for it in underdeveloped places. However, if you think like an improviser, you realize that interesting ideas often come from a dearth of resources or a need to create solutions with very little. A *reverse-innovation* (also known as trickle-up innovation) is an innovation that is either seen first or likely to be used first in the developing world before spreading to the industrialized world. The following story is a great example of the improvisational behaviors in this book. Let's explore how Harman International used improvisational behaviors such as "yes, and," engaged diverse teams, and dealt with the tension of innovation.

Harman International is a U.S.-based company that uses German engineering to create the world's most sophisticated, specialized, and expensive dashboard audiovisual systems. When Dinesh C. Paliwal became CEO in 2007, Harman dominated 70 percent of the luxury car market, which accounted for two-thirds of the company's revenue—not much growth potential there. Paliwal saw a huge opportunity in emerging markets, where Harman's products were virtually nonexistent. However, instead of doing what most high-end companies did, which was simply strip down their existing technology to try to sell at lower cost (which would still have been too expensive, not to mention hardly functional), Paliwal put together a team to reimagine how to deliver a great experience at a low cost for new customers. A natural improviser, Paliwal might have said of emerging markets, "Yes, that's a possibility, and I wonder how we could serve them." He also turned over the stereotype that better is more expensive, and challenged his team to change their point of view.

The initiative was called Saras (which in Sanskrit means "adaptable"), and it was entirely different from anything Harman had done before. The new team was small and cross-functional, rather than highly specialized like Harman's other large, singularly focused engineering teams. It mixed skills, education, and nationalities, and was located in an emerging market rather than an industrialized office in the United States or Germany. The team also set ridiculous goals, such as creating an infotainment system that had all the functionality of their luxury systems at half the price and a third of the cost.

Sounds gutsy, right? And craziest of all, it ended up working. That was thanks to Paliwal's flexibility and improvisational capability to nurture the creative front end of development despite lots of mistakes and restarts, and the tenacity to support the difficult process of getting the innovation manufactured and out to market.

It's difficult to imagine the resistance the Saras team met along the way. Suspicious engineers hated the work and said it would ruin the company's reputation as a high-quality provider. They refused to contribute, so the Saras team hired new, highly diverse engineering talent who didn't have preconceived notions of what could and couldn't be done. They threw them together as a team—and the difficulty galvanized them.

Once the product was ready, salespeople balked and refused to sell the systems because they feared it would cannibalize their commissions. At one point, the chief technology officer even led a coup to kill the entire project and unseat Paliwal. He was unsuccessful and was rousted himself. Through it all, Paliwal and his team kept exhibiting the behaviors of great improvisers. They said "yes, and" to ideas, learned from their mistakes, understood that innovation is an arduous process, and stayed open and supportive. By late spring 2011, Saras had generated more than $3 billion in revenue and set new standards for serving both ends of the market successfully (Govindarajan 2012).

The irony is that the very term *reverse-innovation* implies innovation can only come from a developed market and flow downward to an emerging market. The ego inherent in expensive, developed ideas is that "we are the best." Or that a company must reverse their thinking to get out of their assumptions that "high quality" and "customized" is best. Yet Saras, the low-end, scrappy innovator, redefined what could be delivered. The creativity of lower-end, emerging markets taught the developed markets a thing or two. You don't have to be rich and own a luxury car to get a great sound system in your vehicle. By reversing our assumptions and letting go of ego and hierarchy, we can innovate in the most unexpected ways.

The story of Paliwal and Harmon is a testament to the victory of improvisation and innovation. It wasn't easy, but they didn't give up. That tension between creativity and execution is daunting. But it doesn't mean we can't do this. We can integrate and exhibit the behaviors of improvisation, leading to greater innovation for ourselves, our teams, and our companies.

"The greater the contrast, the greater the potential. Great energy only comes from a correspondingly great tension of opposites."

—Carl Jung

Case Study: Law Firm in the Southwest

My company, ImprovEdge, was once hired to consult with a law firm that realized there was a problem in its initial client engagements. It was losing cases to other firms or discovering key information late in the legal process because clients weren't sharing everything the lawyers needed to know.

The managing partner, who was about to tear out his hair, told me: "We cannot afford to learn critical information about a case two weeks before it goes to trial! Not to mention I just found out another law firm, which is not nearly as qualified as we are and is more expensive, just won out over us! What is going on?"

The situation was becoming critical, and no one seemed able to figure out what was happening. We decided to look at the most tactical possibilities: Could it be caused by their communication style?

When we attended those critical first meetings and observed the attorneys, we were astonished by the clients' body language. While they began the meeting leaning in or speaking quickly, they slowly drew in on themselves, sat back, and crossed their arms. Although the attorneys were there to uncover information, they brought an internal and verbal critic with them. As the clients disclosed details about their problem, the attorneys often jumped in, telling them what they had done wrong. Their responses were peppered with negative words. The clients were there to find solutions to extremely emotional situations, but instead felt as though *they* were on trial.

I surveyed some of the potential clients who had met with the firm. As I spoke to one man leaving his first meeting, he whispered to me, "They certainly are tough, which is something I'll need. But I just don't think they care about how difficult this is for my family. And I had no idea I'd been so dumb about my document preparation. I'm not an attorney! I did the best I could!" He did not hire the firm.

These well-meaning attorneys were bringing risk-aversion, negativity, and a need to show their superiority to their initial client meetings. But their clients wanted a partner in something as scary as a legal battle. They wanted to know someone had their back, understood their mistakes, and had answers.

We took the attorneys through improv sessions that focused on "yes, and," leaning into discomfort, and having creative, collaborative conversations. After that, the firm instituted a five-minute, improvisational "yes, and" period for all first meetings. The attorneys were asked to listen and respond to the client's comments with, "Yes, I bet that was really hard! And then what happened?" or, "Yes, I understand why you chose that action. And I'd like to know more about the other person's response." Those positive, open-ended comments drew in the clients and allowed them to feel heard without criticism.

Once that initial listening and encouragement period was over, the attorneys and clients were able to enter into a collaborative conversation and brainstorm about next steps. We found that the amount of time the client spoke in these new meetings more than doubled. One small office of the firm won $750,000 in extra work in the first six months of instituting this simple, straightforward improvisational technique.

If attorneys—who are intentionally educated to fear risk, apply the brakes, and say "no" as often as possible—can do this, you can too!

Exercise: How We Learn

This exercise is meant to get you or your team out of the comfort zone. Patterns can be stifling, and the simple act of changing a few small things can refresh your viewpoint and allow you to start experiencing things in a new way. This is a first step to taking on larger changes in behavior to drive innovation.

Children's brains are fantastic sponges. They learn with color, music, gooey clay, pets, and constant interaction. Ironically, adults struggle to learn new things and yet we choose less engaging ways to learn. Neuroscientists are also finding that failing to challenge our brains may increase our risk of serious consequences, such as late-life dementia. So let's move away from our sterile lecture environments, interject creativity into our professional lives, exercise our brains, and try new things. After all, it's good for our health and our careers.

- Think about the materials and modes that you use to work and learn. Are they the same ones you've been using for years?

- Acquire things that will force you to document your work differently, such as an artist's notebook, colored pens, books about other industries or interests, a camera, or crossword puzzles.

- Consider how you express yourself. Do you always write in paragraphs, speak in statistics, or present in PowerPoint? Try a completely different tactic such as mind-mapping, telling stories or anecdotes, or engaging in a group exercise rather than a lecture. If you use social media a great deal, take a full day (or week) off. What happens? Conversely, if you don't understand or avoid social media, get an account and spend time learning how it works.

- Integrate different ways to learn into your everyday life. Take lessons on an instrument, go on a field trip with your work group, or try playing a new game. It may be uncomfortable at first, and it probably won't be perfect. But you will start to see things differently and find new talents in yourself. You'll also give your brain a much-deserved workout.

Adventures With Innovation and Improvisation

It's fun to think about the personification of concepts, and that's what we're doing in the comic strip that runs at the end of each chapter. Improvisation embodies many of the aspects of the art form I love: He's goofy, rough around the edges, and open to play. On the other hand, I see Innovation as a smart, sharp, incredibly effective leader.

Preparing Like an Improviser

People might think that improvisers just show up at the theater, pull creative ideas out of their heads, and engage in perfectly timed scenes using only their sheer inborn talent. Not true. Improvisers rehearse, practice, and repeat games over and over. They are constantly working on their characters.

When I first started doing improv in the late eighties, rap was coming to the forefront of music. Anything new in art or culture is immediately nabbed by improvisers, and they try to integrate it into their work. Rap is complicated if done well, and a fellow troupe member made it a goal to master the form. He rapped all day long about every-thing he was doing—whether he was folding laundry, grabbing the bus, or getting ready for a show, he was rapping about it. He recognized that he couldn't wing it; to represent a rapper onstage with real respect, he had to do the work up front.

That's what this chapter is about: the up-front work. There's a lot that goes into creating innovative environments and behaviors in a team or organization or just for yourself. Innovators are tenacious—a lot of time, hard work, and failure will occur before the big breakthrough. Let's examine some of the classic up-front formats and foundations for good, innovative work.

Building Better Brainstorming

Brainstorming is widely held as a key component of getting ideas out onto the table. It's seen as a great exercise and an important piece of engaging your team. Creativity and brainstorming are how we get to innovation. Great inventions and improvements often start at the brainstorming table, so why do so many brainstorming sessions feel useless? Or start with a bang only to yield nothing? No surprise here—it's about our behaviors before, during, and after.

Some descriptions of brainstorming sessions I've heard include:

- "We threw out about 20 ideas each, they were written up on a board, then time was over so we walked out and did nothing."
- "I had an early idea, but my manager said we'd never have the budget and it wouldn't work. So, I didn't add anything else."
- "No way am I sharing my best ideas with the group. I need those to get ahead."
- "Some ideas seemed stupid and had nothing to do with the project."
- "Two people commanded the whole conversation and kept throwing out ideas so no one else could contribute."

That's frustrating talk! Wasted time, unheard ideas, and uneven contributions. Some modern experts consider brainstorming, which was introduced in 1948 by advertising executive and author Alex Osborn, to be good in terms of the need for group process, but awful in terms of method. Fear of failure or judgment and looking after one's own interests are the key reasons we disengage during brainstorming.

Being aware of the strengths and pitfalls of brainstorming can turn that around. Good brainstorming is a critical tool in the pocket of every project team and manager. The key is to understand the nature of effective brainstorming. You must ban the devil's advocate, go for the ridiculous, and embrace the lull.

Ban the Devil's Advocate

The first issue with effective brainstorming is that we must stop allowing the critic to attend. You know the one I'm talking about—the devil's advocate. The moment someone throws on the cloak of the devil's advocate, I want to scream. It means this person is couching criticism and idea-killing comments in the guise of the concerned editor.

We forget how detrimental criticism can be. Contributing in any scenario is very scary for many people. Even those who've worked together for years report putting on a more careful, professional head at work—one that tells them to wait, not say anything, and don't get into trouble. If they believe a comment will be shot down or criticized in any way, they usually choose not to speak. That's narrowing the field of ideas considerably.

The issue is bigger than we may realize. Depending on the setting, normally verbose people can have anxiety in small group sessions. Researchers at Virginia Tech and the journal *Philosophical Transactions of the Royal Society* B found through MRI scans that anxiety affected some people's ability to access their IQ—making them feel dumb, tongue-tied, and worried. Those feelings worsened when they thought others in the group knew more or told them why their ideas wouldn't work (Bernstein 2012).

Don't underplay the importance of all forms of criticism. Rolling your eyes, a sneer, or a silent shrug will do just as much harm as a verbal comment. Body language is loud, and as a leader or member of a team, you have a responsibility to make the brainstorming room safe, creative, and open.

The writer and teacher John Cage created a list of principles for great writing. If you are worried about the critic attending your next brainstorming session, try posting his eighth rule on the wall:

Rule #8: Do not try to create and analyze at the same time. They are different processes.

Brainstorm first. Analyze on a different day.

The More Ridiculous, the Better

I watch executives pull their hair out trying to get their teams to think of something crazy. But even though we all love to say, "The crazy idea may be the best," humans are risk averse. Crazy ideas scare us, and committing a budget to something weird can be a career-limiting move. So the team may be too afraid to take a risk, even in a theoretical brainstorming session.

To loosen up that fear and practice the art of accepting craziness, we use an improvisational brainstorming game called the Ad(d) Game. It requires players to suspend disbelief and commit to a ridiculous idea. They must market a household object with an attribute so weird and unexpected that it is almost unusable in its traditional form: a vacuum cleaner that blows dirt instead of sucking it up or a car with no wheels.

The improvisational aspect of this game is that the participants have to use "yes, and" in their brainstorm and accept every idea to its full potential. As the game progresses, the players enthusiastically plan a rollout of their ridiculous product, complete with pricing, packaging, media plan, celebrity endorsement, and consumer targets. And no matter how ridiculous the idea, every contribution in the brainstorm is greeted with a rousing chorus of "yes, and!"

You can imagine how loud, fun, and crazy this exercise can become. I've seen two extremes of behavior over hundreds of times running this exercise with teams from steelworkers to media CEOs. Ninety-eight percent of teams jump into the game, utterly suspend disbelief, commit with energy, and come up with ideas that are so surprising and brilliant, I'm ready to run out and buy that wheel-less car. Conversely, 2 percent insist the exercise is silly and come up with the most boring ideas I've ever heard. They allow the critic to attend, spending more time arguing than creating. And without fail, those in the latter group do not innovate.

While I have a huge amount of respect for professional marketing and creative teams, my experience shows that they are among the lowest performers in the area of sheer creativity in the Ad(d) Game. Ideas are their stock in trade, and having control of the creative process is a matter of professional pride. I believe they run into a crisis of control—the game can be messy and uncoordinated. Any expert in any field wants to have the best answer—in the case of the Ad(d) Game, I think that need keeps creatives from letting go and just playing the game.

So, what's the point of going for crazy and shutting down the critic? It immediately widens the field of possibility. Although the craziest ideas may not be usable, they expand the breadth of the applied ideas. If you're playing it safe in a limited field of ideas, the chosen ideas (usually in the middle) will remain mundane. If you have a huge field that ranges from mundane to unbelievable, you will probably make connections and see possibilities that are far more interesting.

And sometimes, the most ridiculous and crazy ideas end up being the ones we needed all along. For example, consider a power plant being constructed in Copenhagen by Danish architect Bjarke Ingels' firm, BIG. As the architects and planners brainstormed about the environment, someone noted that there's nowhere to ski in Copenhagen. They joked about putting a ski slope on the power plant. A ridiculous idea, right? Ingels said, "We proposed it as a brainstorm as a joke, but then, you know, it wasn't so silly, and we started like, why would this not be a good idea?" (Bobkoff 2014).

Very soon, you'll be able to take a lift to the top of the power plant, and ski down.

> "I can't understand why people are frightened of new ideas. I'm frightened of the old ones."
>
> —John Cage

Embrace the Lull

Another issue in driving creativity in brainstorming is ending ideation too soon. I call it "the lull." I see it whenever we play the Ad(d) Game.

There's some unavoidable discomfort playing the Ad(d) Game. People are nervous to be up in front of their colleagues, and there is so much fear of being judged. But the exercise always snowballs once participants realize they'll always be greeted by an enthusiastic shout of "yes, and!" The energy is so infectious; audience members join in the fun and start shouting ideas to the volunteers onstage.

However, at some point, there's a lull. Ideas run out, and silence stretches into the room. The participants always look at me, as if to say, "We're done, facilitator. Aren't you going to let us off the hook?" But I don't. I make eye contact, smile encouragingly, and wait for them to start up again. It's slow, and you can practically see their brains working. But this is the point when the million dollar ideas show up and people begin blurting out unexpected combinations and ideas.

By its nature, brainstorming creates obvious outcomes at first. We say everything that pops into our heads. We have to get the easy stuff out of the way before we really start to innovate. It's not until after the lull that groups come up with something kooky, unexpected, and sometimes brilliant. Persistence, discomfort, and sticking with it is a big part of that next step. And in the space of the lull, really creative ideas begin to formulate.

Adam Grant, author and professor at the Wharton School of Business, in his research on the people and teams who seem to come up with the most original, unexpected, and successful innovations, considers the lull an aspect of slowing down and procrastination. In the majority of subjects he studied, procrastination was a constant element in the innovative process for outliers, which he dubbed "Originals." These Originals were natural procrastinators; although they would investigate, study, and think, they resisted solid action until the very last minute. It's funny to hear how their habits drove the author, a self-proclaimed "PREcrastinator" (someone who is driven to do everything early and right away) absolutely crazy! It doesn't make sense, and seems so impractical to people of action. However, he realized that an important synthesis was going on during procrastination.

Grant cites Martin Luther King Jr.'s famous "I Have a Dream" speech as another example of the power of procrastination. King did not finish writing that speech before he gave it, and was making changes up to the last minute—this is where preparation, teamwork, the lull, and improvisation come together.

King had been using his "I have a dream" refrain over the last year, but had removed it from this speech in his notes. As he stood on the steps of the Lincoln Memorial speaking from his prepared text, Mahalia Jackson, legendary gospel singer and King confidante, must have realized he had more—more passion and more energy. Remembering what may have been her favorite refrain, she called out to King, "Tell them about the dream!" In the midst of his speech, King paused, abandoned the script, and improvised. And in that moment of improvisation, he pulled out four brilliant words he had been preparing for more than a year, and "I have a dream" became history.

Grant's realization became complete when he remembered the Zeigarnik effect. Bluma Zeigarnik, a Russian psychologist, found that when people were interrupted during a task, they remembered that task. But they forgot about tasks that were complete. Whenever we finish something, our brain essentially checks it off a list and forgets about it because it needs the space for things that are still in action. Yet, when we leave something unfinished, the brain never stops working on it. It's always a sort of open file, even if it is relegated to the subconscious. The brain can't help but continue working on it (Grant 2016a, 2016b).

That's what happens in the lull! The brain has done a little work, and wants to be let off the hook. However, if we allow the lull to stretch out, even into days or weeks, if the brain understands that there is still work to be done, that work will continue.

In improvisation, that sense of the lull comes from patience. We are always trying out new characters and ideas; we let them brew and don't bring them out again until the time is right. Then one day—BAM! Something really brilliant happens onstage. Our lull can be developing a character over months or respecting the lull that happens in the middle of a show.

I will never forget the difference I saw between improvisers who embraced the lull and those who plowed through it during an improv show in NYC's East Village. Four groups performed that night: three new groups and the house team. It's understood on weeknights the audience only pays a small admission price to see improv by people just learning the craft, as long as they also get a little bit from the pros. I'd rate the first three groups that night from OK to mediocre—they hit a few good moments, but the single attribute that ran through all three was a propensity to rush. They were nervous, dying for a laugh, and wanting to be that combination of energetic, fast, and funny that so many people associate with improv. They were whipping through scenes so quickly that we couldn't keep track of what was going on in the story! And because they were also working so hard, they kept speaking over one another and negating something someone else had just said because they weren't listening.

Then, like a long yoga breath, the house team finally performed. They embraced the lull in a way that felt like relief for us—the confused audience who'd just been hammered by such rushed, loud improv. The team arrived onstage in silence, and seeing that the audience was leaning forward, curious, and engaged, they didn't even speak for the first two to three minutes. Instead, they watched one another as they began to make the actions of eating. When an improviser starts a silent action onstage, her troupe members watch closely so that when they join in, it will work. Slowly, they used their actions to show us and one another that they were eating noodles. As you may imagine, pantomiming the weird stuff that can happen while eating noodles is funny, even without dialogue!

From there, they contributed lines, just one at a time, that were dry and surprising. Whenever a line would catch the audience off guard and we'd laugh, the troupe would let the laughter grow and die down, and would then luxuriate in the next lull. It was like an improvised Samuel Beckett play. They'd acknowledge the new information, think about it quietly, eat their noodles, and wait for the right line to come . . . which it did, again and again. Those noodle eaters explored work, sex, and love in matter-of-fact tones of voice while they slowly put away their lunchtime noodles. It was one of the most brilliant improv scenes I've enjoyed in years. That one scene took up the entire space of their time slot. There was no need to zip between settings, characters, and time—they luxuriated in lulls and patience to fully explore a hysterical trio of noodle eaters.

Adults dislike discomfort and being outside their area of expertise. And in group situations, we often hate silence. But we must stretch into the unknown. Having the courage to hang on through the lull is critical. Sometimes the lull is a break, a moment of relaxation when we access different areas of our brain and an idea arrives. Sometimes it's just believing that there's more, and not giving up. I sometimes wonder how many great ideas were left unsaid because we bailed out of an uncomfortable lull.

Environment

Why does environment matter to improvisation and innovation? The physical environment isn't the only thing that affects our behaviors; the resources and personal interactions that occur in our environment also deeply affect our efficacy.

From a foundational perspective, researchers continue finding links to our efficacy and success based on our childhood environments. How and where we are raised and nurtured has so much to do with what we accomplish later in life. For example, economists have found that access to good public transportation and manageable commute times are key indicators in escaping poverty and gaining upward mobility (Chetty and Hendren 2015). Sadly, it has been found that even if impoverished kids have better test scores, two parents, and a lower crime rate near their home, if they don't have access to reliable transportation to get in and out of their neighborhood, they'll have less chance of moving up and out of poverty than those who do. That single lever influences their success so much.

There are many levers that can affect your team's ability to improvise and innovate. The key is to look around, question, and try things that could improve outcomes from an environmental perspective. This is a front-end effort because if the environment doesn't work, how can we? The critical importance of environment cannot be underplayed—if the environment is conducive to creativity, your brain will be better able to focus and innovate. In addition, environment affects our behaviors, which is exactly what we are trying to unleash.

Take this professional services firm located in a small Midwestern town, for example. All the offices in this classic, historical stone building are private, and the abundance of carpet, walls, and narrow hallways encourage quiet work and isolation. Every office is dominated by a big oak desk or table, so that people are separated by a piece of furniture when they sit down, and it's difficult to have a seating configuration other than facing off across a desk. If people from the same department work on different floors, they rarely see each other. Admins must walk across the building or to different floors to talk to a teammate, and may not see each other in a whole week.

The firm determined that they could save money and be more productive if administrative assistants could collaborate and share more work, but there are no spaces large enough to build a team area. While email, text, instant message, and videoconference may help, such an environment–common for early-20th-century work–is problematic for modern collaboration. What could the firm do?

Actually, quite a bit. The firm decided to rethink how it worked, and deal with the constraints as a conduit for creativity rather than a barrier. For example, there was a library that took up most of the first floor, but it wasn't really necessary with so much information available online. So, the library was transformed into a gathering and conference space with a coffee bar, reception area, and many informal spots for small, in-the-moment meetings. Admins, executives, and support staff could now mix in a way that allowed much more social and professional interaction. In addition, the support staff was consolidated on the basement floor–which was refurbished and reconfigured for light, access, and color–where they could be near each other and collaborate quickly. Most impressive, the firm reconsidered its entire strategy. By reconfiguring reporting, office, and work structures, it was able to work as a team more effectively and serve its clients more efficiently.

This was all accomplished because the firm decided to approach its restrictive environment as creatively as possible. By contrast, let's consider an innovation lab set up by Cardinal Health in Columbus, Ohio.

Built out from the expansive shell of a former grocery store, the lab, Fuse, was deliberately designed to be an environment that encouraged collaboration and open ideation. There were no offices or assigned desks. Instead, people simply chose a quiet spot or a place in the open theater area near their current project teammates. The conference rooms are designated by colors chosen to compliment certain sorts of brain activity: red for intense discussion, speed, and co-creation; blue for project planning and consideration; green for focused work and productivity; and orange for sharing and creative play. Magnetized walls and dozens of rolling whiteboards are covered with notes, pictures, designs, and plans, and were meant to move and change with the activities and ideas they document. Interactive screens and video monitors stream key information into the conversation each day. And suspended from the ceiling are toys and other playful artifacts that represent the spirit of various teams and projects.

The mix of professional skills throughout the environment is also very deliberate. The diversity in expertise and close proximity build respect and help spark ideas that would simply never catch fire in a regimented, cube-walled office. Each day, quick stand-up meetings keep everyone current on the work being done in the lab within and across different teams. Employees are encouraged to eat together (on actual plates with silverware) at a sprawling family table called "the Hub" and frequent pot-luck events foster even more community. Once a week, in a labwide stand-up meeting, employees share accomplishments and announcements, and then everyone pitches in to do a quick clean-up of the desktops and common areas—almost like a family. The space feels like an active part of the collaborative culture and seems to say, "We are all accountable, we are all in this together."

These stories are meant to inspire you to think creatively about preparing and changing your environment. Putting Fuse together was an act of deliberate innovation. However, if you find yourself in an environment more like the professional services firm, ask yourself what you can do to prepare like an improviser. If your physical space is restrictive, what can you change, even if it is small? What behaviors can you introduce that will change the way your team interacts with the environment?

In an improv show, we tend to work in small theaters, close to the audience. We even tear down the metaphysical fourth wall to make the entire audience part of the show. The *fourth wall* (a term from classical theater) refers to the idea that there's an invisible fourth wall on the stage that keeps the actors separate from audience. They are entirely immersed in their characters in the time and place the script dictates. But in improv, we look right at the audience, speak with them, and even bring them onstage from time to time.

When participants walk into one of my ensemble's improv workshops, the first thing they see is an open semicircle of chairs. That, in and of itself, often makes them very uncomfortable. They likely expected to come into a room full of tables, where they could set up their laptops in the back, stay out of the spotlight, and zone out for the training. That open room lets them know there will be no hiding. Being asked to improvise puts many people way outside their comfort zone. The key is creating a safe space for them where there are no mistakes, people volunteer rather than being told or chosen to engage, and everyone has a chance to contribute. We are all in it, together.

Environment matters. What culture and physical attributes are in yours?

Preparation and Practice

The adage "luck is when opportunity meets preparation" refers to the fact that many humble people have said that they owe their big break to "luck." As if anyone could have achieved that same moment, if only all the stars aligned in the same way. Not true. The *Merriam-Webster Dictionary* defines luck as "the things that happen to a person because of chance: the accidental way things happen without being planned." However, when people work very hard, prepare a great deal, or practice incessantly—so that when the moment comes and the agent or CEO is in the room, they perform perfectly—the "luck" that put the right person there pays off because they rock the house.

Preparation is a huge part of dealing with challenges. Every athlete knows that if you don't put in the time to practice, sweat, fail, get up, start over, and try again, you'll never reach the physical skills and endurance it takes to be great. Practice is an obvious and entirely expected part of their excellence. So why do we think we can be creative or innovative without dedicating our own sweat and practice?

If you want to be a more creative person, engage in small creative behaviors. Do small things every day, practice the art of creativity, and innovate in ways that seem very household. Give your brain a chance to create new neural pathways, and give your body and emotions the chance to engage in failure, challenge, and retry. As long as you are comfortable and totally in your zone of expertise, you are probably stagnating!

Case Study: Global Medical Device Company

Ben had a challenge ahead of him. As a senior scientist and vice president of a global medical device company, he had just received the green light to move forward on an innovative project that could revolutionize the way medical tests are conducted in automated clinical labs. He had the audacious goal of creating a machine that could produce outcomes on clinical medical tests (such as cervical cancer) in less time and in significantly higher numbers than ever before.

This high-throughput instrument allows clinical laboratories to screen many more women for cervical cancer. That's a huge improvement in medical outcomes. But that wasn't all—the company wanted him to complete this project in less than half the time they usually allowed.

Ben is a man with enormous good humor, which would be critical in the next few years. He told me about the challenge: "There are so many eyes on this project! We got a great budget, but everyone is wondering if we can make this happen. We have to totally reconsider how we collaborate as a team, build devices, and serve the client. Everything is changing."

Instead of diving right in, Ben knew that a lot of up-front work had to happen to achieve this innovation. His main concern rested on two very simple communication behaviors: speaking up and clarifying. He had led teams for many years and had observed a persistent and problematic set of behaviors in the company—a reticence to speak up in rooms with people who were higher-ranking and an avoidance of asking questions.

For example, if a team was reviewing its work on a scientific project, people in the room wouldn't want to bring negative news and were worried that they didn't have the rank to speak in meetings, even though the team leader asked about any issues that may have arisen during testing. So, while they would explain the issue to their peers after the meeting, it could take another week for the issue to come around to the team leader. That is a huge amount of time wasted, which Ben knew he didn't have for this new project. In addition, if team members did not understand, they would go off and do their own research, and then take action on what they learned. That often led to issues simply because they didn't clarify their actions.

"I've even found out that members of my own team won't challenge me in front of others, when I'm begging them to do so!" he explained to me. "My simplest measure of success is even one person speaking up immediately who normally would have stayed quiet. Right there, we could save a week of time—and we need every single minute we can spare on this project."

It may seem surprising that these behaviors were being exhibited by extremely smart, highly educated scientists. However, anyone can feel intimidated, shy, and reticent. If you work in an environment where no one else seems to be engaging in certain behaviors, such as clarifying with questions, you will avoid those as well. You'll just nod with understanding like everyone else.

Ben wanted to create a completely different environment. He needed to prepare his team for this intense experience, which would be short and reliant upon radical collaboration. He needed an improv troupe.

And so, ImprovEdge engaged the team in a series of workshops, webinars, coaching sessions, and internal cohort work organized around improvisational behaviors. We taught the team about "yes, and," so that they could question and confirm their intelligence: "Yes, I appreciate the explanation, and I'd like to know more about the third component."

We also discussed culture and environment—what interactions could allow them to feel more comfortable? We created formats for everyone to speak up in brainstorming sessions, so that lower-level employees would become comfortable with adding their voices to all interactions. High-level leadership attended all sessions, encouraging everyone to contribute, speak, add ideas to the table, and work together.

We taught them specific communication tools such as reflections (What I hear you saying is . . .), open-ended questions (Could you tell me some more about . . . ?), and ideation. And yes! The team played the Ad(d) Game many times to explore the lull, getting through everyone's ideas, and contributing quickly. One junior project manager told us, "The level of trust I feel with this team after the sessions is incredible! It's higher than anything I felt at my last company after three years. I think the fact that we all had to step out of our comfort zone together is what made the difference. My superiors were just as nervous as I was—but we all had fun! And the techniques work, too. Just yesterday, I brainstormed with my VP—we never would have even chatted before this."

One of the most telling success stories came from a woman on the team for whom English was a second language. After learning how to use reflections, she told the entire group that she had implemented that simple technique for clarification. "When I started to reflect back on what I thought I heard, so many people clarified for me. I have realized that I probably have been misunderstanding about 50 percent of what I've been hearing from all of you. I was scared to tell you this, but my team member encouraged me to let you all know so we can work together to help me understand everything more quickly."

She realized that by pushing through her shyness and reflecting and pausing to set a foundation of understanding, she was speeding up her work significantly. In addition, by reaching out and clarifying, she was building stronger relationships with her team members. Her assumption had been that questioning would push them away, but once she got into more specific conversations, she realized that it was bringing them closer together in camaraderie and understanding.

In another instance, an engineer came to our third workshop with a story about "yes, and":

> I went to visit our vendor partner who is manufacturing a special component for the machine. I was starting to get concerned, because I was confused about the specs he was showing me. I kept questioning him about missing pieces, but he was starting to get defensive and, I would wager, was also starting to think I was an idiot because I didn't seem to understand him. In the past, I might have just ended the meeting, come back, and told the team we may have to reconsider our choice of vendor, which would have been a huge problem. Instead, I took a deep breath and remembered "yes, and." So I stopped for a second, totally changed my tone of voice, and said, "Yes, I see that those four components are right in place. They look great. And as I turn the plans around, I'm confused about the back half. Could you help me see that more clearly?"
>
> The vendor's face lit up. "Oh I get it! The specs don't even show the back half! I'm so sorry. Wow, I can see how that could be confusing. We don't use the mirror image, and I thought you knew that. Here! Let's go out on the manufacturing floor and I'll show you the whole process."

That engineer from Ben's team ended up getting a tour of the whole facility, they had a great conversation, and he saw everything being made and assembled. That meeting launched a much stronger, more communicative relationship with the vendor.

The outcome of this up-front improvisational work for the project was enormous. By setting a foundation and environment of improvisation, the team achieved its innovative goals, and Ben included them all when they made their final presentation to the CEO. Most impressive? The first versions of the machines have been built and are currently running thousands of medical tests in R&D labs.

Exercise: Collaborative Brainstorming

This fun, high-energy brainstorming session is about getting ideas and plans into place quickly. By making the event game-like, it allows people to have fun and create a very visual outcome. Their ideas will cover a wall and they'll be timed to create intensity. Finally, multiple teams will engage on how to use and implement ideas.

1. Choose topics or projects that need to be addressed. Create teams of three people, with at least two teams per subject. For example, your company needs to launch a product for a new target market.

2. Carefully consider preparation and environment. You'll need notecards or sticky notes (use large ones for easy writing, nothing tiny) and colored markers, as well as lots of wall space, flipcharts, and of course, snacks! Consider: Is there enough space for the number of people you have invited? Will sticky notes stay on the wall in the room or will you need to tack notecards to the wall? Do the markers work well? Is the room in a place where you can have a noisy session?

3. Assign trios of people to the topics for the collaborative brainstorm. They each have a role: One person is the brainstormer, who thinks and speaks. Another person is the scribe, who writes down everything the brainstormer says—one idea per sticky note. The third person is the organizer, who gathers the outcomes and posts them on the wall.

4. Set a timer for three to five minutes. The brainstormers will come up with ideas around something specific (example: how do we create a new process to roll out the website?) or general (example: what can we do to reach our yearly goals?). As they say each idea, the scribes write it on a sticky, which they hand to the organizers. Since there

are at least two teams per topic, the organizers for each topic work together as a team to create categories for the ideas on the wall as quickly as possible. As they grab ideas and collaborate, columns or areas of sticky notes with common ideas should start to come together. If you are brainstorming multiple topics, put each topic on a separate wall to avoid confusion.

5. Have everyone do a quick, one-minute review of the wall so they know which ideas have already been written down.

6. Now, rotate roles! Do at least two rounds if not three, so that the team members experience each different role. Encourage new ideas and encourage crazy! Remind them that you want to see ridiculous ideas right beside the obvious ones.

7. Work together to eliminate duplicates and organize the wall to create clear categories of ideas for each topic.

8. Once the brainstorming is over, have the groups use flipcharts to strategize how to put the ideas into action. Allow at least 15-20 minutes for conversation and work.

9. Have each team present their ideas to the group. This is an idea session, not an editing session! Keep everything and edit later.

Adventures With Innovation and Improvisation

In the year since we last saw them, Innovation and Improvisation have gone into business together. They chose an office filled with wall space for ideation and lots of room for group interaction. But Innovation worries that her partner's constant playfulness followed by procrastination will sink the ship. Here it is, the night before their first presentation to a venture capital firm, and they still don't have a name for the company!

Improvisation stands by the wall, adding another suggestion to the more than 400 possible names for their company.

Meanwhile Innovation lies on the floor littered with paper, boxes, and supplies thinking about the past year.

They had enjoyed whirlwind activity including focus groups, field trips, interviews, and spreadsheets!

But there were also those long periods of no activity, where Improvisation wouldn't make a decision, and all sorts of deadlines were missed.

During one lull, Improvisation had brought in a group of circus acrobats, and rigged a trapeze for them.

She had seriously considered bailing on the whole thing at that point. But she was amazed how different physics felt when flipping from one trapeze to the next.

Innovation squints up at the ceiling, noticing the pictures and scribbles left by the trapeze artists. She suddenly sits up, dumping a cat onto a nearby beanbag.

FLIP PHYSICS!

Eureka! That's it! Now we can start working!!!

That will be our name!

Playing in
the Moment

Play is a beautiful and critical aspect of improvisation. We rarely say that we are performing. When improvisers get together to rehearse or do a show, we tell people we are getting together to play. "We're playing Friday at 10 p.m.—want to come?" is a common refrain because it's not only the improvisers who play, the audience plays too. We use their suggestions, energy, and comments, and even have them come onstage to shape what we do—we're all in it together.

There's fascinating research about the importance of play to the human and even animal condition. Stuart Brown, in his 2009 book, *Play: How It Shapes the Brain, Opens the Imagination, and Invigorates the Soul,* tracks the evolutionary process of play. He finds that mammals and advanced species need play; it underpins our evolutionary state, survival, brain size, and social structure. Throughout his decades of research, Brown found that murderers often had childhoods devoid of play and fun, while extremely happy professionals never stopped playing. Play is a need for both humans and animals—the anticipation, interaction, competition, pleasure, surprise, and engagement of play is vital because it shows us at our absolute best.

And most telling, Brown contends that the improvisational nature of play allows us to synthesize ideas in unexpected ways. We jump into new ways of thinking and behaving during the act of play, so that suddenly our brain makes connections that wouldn't otherwise be found. He gives the example of an engineer building sandcastles at the beach. While playing with her children in the sand, the engineer may stumble upon an insight for her work.

To understand how play can inform and affect our lives, let's look at some of the elements of play and improvisation. Rather than looking at the obvious elements, such as competition, that are so richly explored by Brown and his colleagues, I want to explore aspects of play that are more intuitive and improvisational: focus, team, commitment, and doing stuff. These are all behaviors of both improvisation and innovation.

"This is the real secret of life—to be completely engaged with what you are doing in the here and now. And instead of calling it work, realize it is play."

—Alan W. Watts

Focus!

One of the most enjoyable aspects of play is the focus that takes over during acts of play. We become absorbed, lose track of time, and are utterly focused on what is happening right here in the moment. In improv, focus is critical to creating a great show. When people who have never improvised play improv games, they often talk about their heightened state of attention and listening. They are in the midst of something they've never done before, they want to do well, and they have no idea what's going to happen next. Even when the control freaks try to direct a game, they soon learn it's impossible, drop their preconceived notions, and simply play the game. It's critical to be in the moment.

Unfortunately, we are rarely in the moment in our day-to-day lives. As adults, we spend most of our time elsewhere—we're always thinking about things like what we had for breakfast or what we should do tomorrow or the next day. Even when we're having an intense debate, we stop listening to the other person and start thinking about our rebuttal, or how smart we'll sound when we give a snappy comeback, or we'll become so distracted thinking about our next meeting that we zone out. It is very difficult to be in the moment. But one of the most important behaviors of innovative people is the ability to focus, be in the now, and watch without preconceived notions.

On the improv stage, we call it scriptwriting when someone stops being in the moment. It's a serious no-no. Everybody else onstage can tell when someone is thinking ahead and trying to control where the show is going. It's usually because that person has had a "brilliant" idea and wants to make sure the story goes in the direction he imagines. It's a disaster! He cuts off scenes, tells other people onstage who they are, and basically bullies the work. The sense of play dies, and even the audience can sense that something is wrong.

Improv is great because it is in the moment. You have to roll with whatever the ensemble throws out, and when you can connect and add a great character, joke, or song to the moment on stage, they'll roll with it, too. It's an amazing, symbiotic experience that I've rarely experienced elsewhere.

The all-consuming act of improvisation (creation in the moment without preconceived plans) shuts down the critics in our brain. It's beautiful, really. I love the image of the wizened pundit, the one that seethes doubt and self-consciousness, bound and gagged in a corner while the creative artist/scientist part of the brain is off spinning with abandon. So often the critic introduces self-doubt and fear so that the artist/scientist is unable to experiment. Focus shuts out the mean-spirited voice in our heads.

So how do we enter this state of improvisation? True improvisation occurs when years of experience allow a performer, athlete, musician, scientist—or you—to enter a mixed state of conscious and subconscious. When a person knows so much about a subject or has done something for so long that it's no longer entirely conscious, they can go "off script." They begin creating, dancing, or speaking a foreign language without the need to plan. The idea is to take the reins off your brain, and allow it to focus and run. When you can go deeply into a subject, you can begin to improvise with what you know, creating new pathways, new processes, new innovations. Improvisation is a beautifully deep and absorbing process, and one that your brain already knows how to accomplish.

Being in the moment is light. You've probably felt it when you've looked up and suddenly realized that you were absorbed, you had left the world of care or preoccupation, and it's much later than you imagined. Something had taken over and you had created or done a task or watched something beautiful.

Those experiences feel all too rare thanks to distraction and multitasking. Those pernicious problems are the inverse, the enemy of being in the moment.

There are many stories about interruption and distractions ruining the playful, creative process. One of the most famous is Samuel Taylor Coleridge's unexpected caller. Once the poet awoke from an opium-induced sleep with exotic images in his head and immediately set about writing "Kubla Khan," a poem of fantasy and sensuality. Unexpectedly, a man he forevermore called a "person from Porlock" interrupted his work by happening along. When Coleridge returned to the page, he couldn't write any more. He reported having the feeling for the rest of his life that the poem was in his head, but he was never able to access it again to finish it (Poetry Foundation 2016).

Multitasking is another terrible enemy to focus. The past decade has produced study after study proving the cognitive detriment of multitasking. Even the youngest generation—those born into the electronic, multitasking world—are suffering. As Devora Zack (2015) outlined in her lighthearted yet science-packed book, *Singletasking,* "College and high school students have the same memory limitations as adults. . . . We understand and recall less when task-shifting. . . . Learning to concentrate is a life skill." She goes further to quote a Harvard study (Junco and Cotten 2012) that revealed divided attention and multitasking behavior "leads to a lower capacity for cognitive processing and precludes deeper learning."

Neuroscientists have proven that multitasking is indeed impossible. The belief that a person can accomplish several things at a time is a myth. Not to mention that every time the brain switches between tasks, the quality of the work and focus degrades (Ophir et al. 2009).

Even more alarming is the documented reality that by overloading our brains with stress, we are actually shrinking our brains! When we multitask, the amygdala, the ancient little piece of our brain at the base of the neck that is responsible for fight, flight, and freeze, floods the prefrontal cortex with cortisol, the stress hormone. The prefrontal cortex, where we do our high-level thinking and cognition, becomes impaired by this constant overdose, and the brain begins to shrink, lose capacity to function, and be effective (Laubach 2011).

So, if we're turning our brains to mush, what does that mean for the future of our inventions, our great novels, our disease-killing drugs?

Your brain wants to focus. It's dying for a little fun time to go deeply into a single issue and play around without restriction. And improvisation is the answer. Fortunately, the brain already knows how to take care of itself; it simply requires us to enter a state of focus and improvisation. In 2010, Aaron Berkowitz and Daniel Ansari studied the brain activity of musicians and nonmusicians, and found that when improvising, highly trained musicians entered a different chemical state. Using MRI scans, the researchers found that the musicians' brains shut down the temporo-parietal junction, which allows your attention to be distracted by peripheral stimulus like a shiny object, movement, sound, or color. In addition, there was a surge of medial prefrontal activity, where expressiveness occurs in the brain, and the lateral prefrontal regions—the areas that control inhibition and self-consciousness—were shut down.

"In other words," wrote Amanda Rose Martinez (2010) in *Seed* magazine about the researchers, "[in] the improviser's brain, the area that imposes self-restraint powers down, allowing the region that drives self-expression, which ramps up, to proceed virtually unchecked." The amazing thing is that improvisation actually orders the brain to shut down regions of itself that would interfere with the free-flowing process of creation. Distractions are eliminated and self-consciousness is unplugged.

"Men do not quit playing because they grow old; they grow old because they quit playing."

—Oliver Wendell Holmes Sr.

I once worked with a man at an energy provider. He was a safety inspector and had been in the trenches laying lines for years. He was gruff and quiet except when he talked about his favorite hobby, rebuilding vehicles. He specialized in three- and four-wheelers, laughing as he recounted many nights where he "looked up and it was midnight!" He talked about that time in the garage, covered with oil and trying to fix broken vehicle components, as "playtime."

"Even though I've been concentrating on fixing the dune buggies, sometimes I'll walk out and realize I've solved another problem. Something at work—an interpersonal issue or a project I just couldn't get figured out. I think that focused time, without distractions or phone calls, allows my brain to do other work."

Indeed it does. Just as in sleep and in the lull we discussed around brainstorming, allowing the brain to focus on a task and stop multitasking frees up your subconscious capability to think on a higher level.

Teaming Up

One of the misconceptions about innovation is our popular notion that genius is individual. Someone blessed with ability and talent becomes an overnight success through raw talent. You either have it or you don't, and when you do, you're a lone wolf. But the reality is that great innovation, just like great improvisation, happens in groups.

It's funny, but when I tell people I did improv, they assume I mean stand-up comedy. The little stand-up I did wasn't very good, and it filled me with terror. I'm in awe of stand-up, because good or bad, you are out there all alone. In contrast, I couldn't wait to get to my next improv gig because I knew I'd have a team—I'd never be alone onstage, left out to dry, and manage an unhappy crowd by myself. By the same token, if we rocked, I'd have a whole ensemble with whom to celebrate! Every moment of creation felt richer and more alive to me because it was an in-the-moment collaboration. Because we were working together, we could play off the many surprising, creative, and wonderful things that came out of the weird brains of my improv friends. Truth be told, even stand-up performers rarely do all their work alone. They have friends and collaborators, people who watch and give them feedback, and writers who create content for them to deliver. The amazing comedy and creativity that audiences see onstage is the product of intense group collaboration.

Therefore, we need to realign our misconceptions about innovation. It's a group sport, and the greatest innovators act like an improv troupe. Although innovators often drive their ideas with tenacity through hardship, they rarely do it alone. Many people picture famous innovators alone, in their lab coats, being struck by a great idea. However, many of the most famous "loners" were actually surrounded by collaborators.

The very symbol for the big idea, a lightbulb, was invented by Thomas Edison. But he didn't create it by himself. Edison usually worked in a laboratory funded by a corporate sponsor, surrounded by countless scientists, and was said to have more than 30 assistants! The lightbulb only came about through a series of inventions that led to a great breakthrough (Israel 1998).

Steve Jobs was widely described as he was seen during Apple's product launches—alone on a stage, in his iconic black turtleneck, being a genius. He displayed all the same behaviors of play, thinking upside down, and front-end considerations that improvisers do; he also had a team. In addition to Steve Wozniak, he also worked for years with Joanna Hoffman, Bud Tribble, George Crow, Rich Page, and Susan Barnes. Not to mention his huge company of coders, computer scientists, assistants, and designers. The entire ecosystem of Apple was not just about Steve Jobs—it was about creativity and innovation—and it was peopled with hundreds.

Innovation:
- Something new or different introduced.
- The act of innovating; introduction of new things or methods.

Great ideas grow stronger in the right types of groups. If teams engage in improvisational behaviors, their play can enrich the idea and take it places. That sort of ecosystem was explored by Keith Sawyer in his 2007 book *Group Genius*. He examines the percolation of ideas, verbal cues, body language, and incremental changes of groups. The sudden spark of an idea is usually the result of long-term social interaction coming together in a realization. Writes Sawyer: "Innovation today isn't a sudden breakwiththepast,abrilliantinsightthatoneloneoutsiderpushesthrough.... Just the opposite: innovation today is a continuous process of small and constant change, and it's built into the culture of successful companies."

Playing With Nonexperts

There's another key aspect of teams, play, and innovation. It's about leveraging all sorts of people and ideas, not just experts. All those teams of innovators weren't experts right away; they often took inspiration from nonexperts. Steve Jobs resisted overengineered computers because he saw that normal people wanted something simple, not something intimidating and complicated. His customers, not experts, were his litmus test.

One of the reasons improv can be so funny is that we take on characters and situations for which we know nothing! Improv teams usually aren't experts in astronomy, economics, DNA, or pastry baking. Yet we can create funny, touching, and impressive scenes by pulling together the pieces of our knowledge and making a great scene.

I was once in a scene about collecting antique guns. None of us knew much about antique guns; however, Eric had done Civil War reenactments and knew the look and feel of an antique gun, Frances avidly watched *Antiques Roadshow* and had seen an episode on guns once, and I had cleaned my dad's hunting shotguns as a kid. We committed and somehow pulled out a really funny and intricate scene. It was so good, the man who had shouted the suggestion came up after the show, assuming we were also collectors like him. When we told him it was an amalgam of small pieces of information, he was flabbergasted.

"I am looking for a lot of people who have an infinite capacity to not know what can't be done."

—Henry Ford

Anybody can play! And when everybody gets to play, surprising things happen. Another issue in innovation? Leaving all the thinking, ideation, and play to "the best heads in the department." Surrounding yourself with a bunch of experts—or leaving innovation to only a single or small group of experts—is idiocy. The deeper an expert goes into an area of expertise, the less open he is to divergence and possibility. Ironically, in addition to having deep knowledge of their work, subject matter experts may also hold themselves back.

James Surowiecki, in his book *The Wisdom of Crowds* (2004), traces the efficacy of group thinking. He contends that a large group of everyday people often have enough collective wisdom to out-think a guru. The beauty of nonexperts is that they are not hampered by the curse of knowledge, which tends to show up in several ways. First, your knowledge of an area is so deep that you unconsciously skip over steps or details, simply because they are "obvious." That leaves nonexperts bewildered as they try to figure out what you are talking about.

I encountered it the first time I sent a draft of my first book to my editor. She called to let me know there were many passages on improvisation where she had no earthly idea what I was talking about. Improv had become so innate, so obvious and ingrained to me, that I took the small processes completely for granted, to the point where I no longer explained them.

The curse of knowledge also gets in the way by creating boundaries around your knowledge. You'll experience multiple issues, disappointments, and surprising outcomes, which teaches you to be cagey. The more expertise you have, the more issues and boundaries it creates. Sometimes the more you know, the more obstacles you see. Conversely, nonexperts don't know they can't or shouldn't do something. And here's the weird part—those nonexperts, those who are free to believe that something is still possible, might just make it happen.

"In the beginner's mind there are many possibilities; in the expert's mind there are few."

—Shunryu Suzuki

How Much Can Nonexperts Do?

Rice University challenges its students to create inventions that solve third-world problems. One group created a very cheap bubble CPAP (continuous positive airway pressure) machine to use with premature infants born in Malawi, a country with little to no funding for equipment in hospitals and unstable electrical systems. So, the students used a shoebox and two aquarium pumps. Why not? They were not hamstrung by the belief that medical equipment had to be professionally made with expensive materials, as some manufacturers might. The device worked and has started saving infant lives already. These students improvised— they chose to see boundaries as possibilities, and worked together for a goal they believed was achievable (Nye 2014; Palca 2014).

Let everybody play. Innovation is a team sport, just like improvisation. Experts and laypeople both have something to contribute, and their interaction will probably lead to more diverse outcomes. Despite the unwieldy messiness, diverse playmates make for unexpected and often innovative outcomes.

"None of us is as smart as all of us."

—Japanese Proverb

Commitment

For years, I've been attending my children's basketball, soccer, football, cross-country, and baseball events. I can't even count the number of times a coach yelled out, "I need to see some commitment out there!" or "You've got to commit to [choose one] winning/your team/the basket/ the goal/the last 100 yards!" In these instances, commitment is about giving it your all, playing like there is no other option in life, and not holding anything back.

It's the same in improv. There are two key sides to commitment in improvisation: the commitment itself and commitment's ability to allow the audience to suspend their disbelief. When an improviser is so good, so into a character that she looks and sounds like the real thing, the audience will utterly enjoy the show. We all know that she's not an astronaut, a WNBA player, or a spy, but when she commits fully and plays every moment as if it's true, the audience allows their brains to believe. It's a wonderful part of theater, improv, movies, and art. We think, "OK, for the fun of it, I'm going to suspend my skepticism and my logical understanding that this would never happen. It will allow me to believe a tiny woman is playing in the WNBA and enjoy this crazy show!"

Consider action films. There's just no way real human beings could come out of landslides, explosions, and overcome 20 armed enemies. But we choose to believe it, because it's part of the fun, the hope, the beauty of art. You've probably seen movies where they went too far—made it too difficult to suspend your disbelief—and you walked out feeling skeptical, as though the movie makers had insulted your intelligence. But when done right—when they commit to creating a world where we can easily suspend our disbelief—it's magic. And those behaviors allow us to engage in creative and innovative behavior as well.

The concept of commitment in improv is about never pulling back: going with an idea to its fullest extent, even if it feels as though it's not working. Commitment is key to success, because the minute an improviser stops committing, everyone knows: The actor is only sort of playing someone in love or someone obsessed by numbers or a farmer or a garbage collector, so even if he hits funny moments, it's just not as funny. That's because the audience can't suspend its disbelief.

I once saw an improv show on New York's West Side, and the second half was sketch comedy. Sketch is born out of improv. Actors, writers, and directors love to mess around with concepts and stories. So, when they've improvised a few characters or an idea that seems to work, they'll script it and put it into sketch comedy. We call it "sketch" and not "scripted" because although the actors are held to the outcomes and goals of the story, they're free to improvise the lines.

Well, not every night of improv is good. The concept was a family sitcom, but the couple breaks up and decides to do their own shows, each using their son as the foil. It loosely held together character sketches of goofy and weird situations. And it was really bad. While there were funny moments, and I laughed out loud several times, the troupe decided to go with really "wrong" ideas to see if they could pull the comedy out. ("Wrong" is when comedians decide to take on a politically incorrect subject, knowingly play the heck out of the stereotype, and allow the audience to laugh at the fact that they'll do and say what no one else will.) They had a scene about senior citizens addicted to crack, a scene about pedophilia, and another about planning a party for the day after 9/11. Remember, we're in New York City. It bombed. (Pun intended.) It was so bad that I saw one of the actors sneak over to the bar during a break and grab a shot.

I know how it feels to be having a horrible night on stage. Your insides curl up and every time the punchline meets silence your blood gets another degree colder. There have been many times in my career that I wanted a shot of tequila halfway through, too. But guess what? Even though the show was terrible, I was still delighted to watch them. They were the definition of pros. Not once did they falter, not once did they give the scenes less than 100 percent; they even took their bows to tepid applause with huge smiles on their faces. We never saw them sweat. And because of their commitment, I was willing to try again with every scene. Even though they kept hitting rock bottom, when they came out onstage with a new character, utterly engaged and playing it full tilt, I was willing to suspend my disbelief just one more time. They kept me engaged.

You might be thinking, "Well that was a completely wasted night, and who knows how many weeks of rehearsal." But it wasn't. Because they didn't stop committing, they found several great moments in their sketches. They were able to learn what works and what doesn't, and they'll never have to wonder, "Gee, if I'd given it my all, that third joke might have worked." And here's another thing improvisers know—they must have the courage to go back and commit every single time. They probably did that same show again, just to see if it would play better for another audience on another night of the week.

This is directly linked to the people who are creative and innovative every day. Joy Mangano was a single mom who was highly inventive and displayed many of the behaviors of creative and innovative people. Her first idea, a reflective pet flea collar, was a great and new idea for the early 1990s. Unfortunately, she didn't patent the idea and the Hartz Mountain company bought a similar idea and took over the market. Instead of thinking, "I'm not an inventor, I don't even understand patents," Mangano doubled-down on her commitment to be an inventor of things that make life easier. Although she went through a divorce and had to work as a waitress and airline customer service representative to fill the gaps, she kept looking for ideas. Her next big idea, the Miracle Mop, garnered early interest from QVC. She put her entire life savings into manufacturing the new product and made the first 100 in her dad's auto body shop. The movie *Joy*, starring Jennifer Lawrence, chronicles the heart-wrenching moment when a celebrity botched the sale of her mop on TV. QVC calls Mangano to tell her it's too bad, but the mop is a flop, good-bye.

She could have said, "A big, important celebrity couldn't sell my mop, and QVC says it's not a good product. I'd better bow out, because they know more than I do, and I've already lost most of my assets!" But instead of folding or pulling back, Mangano committed. She insisted that QVC allow her to show the mop on TV herself. And it's true, when Mangano, an ordinary mom, appeared on TV to sell the mop, she committed to the product and the moment because it was everything she had, and she knew it would work. Her total believability allowed thousands of people to suspend their disbelief that this new product might be a scam or might not work. On that first appearance, Mangano sold 18,000 units in less than half an hour. She now holds the patents to more than 100 inventions, and eventually sold her company, Ingenious Designs, to the Home Shopping Network. HSN continued to cash in; Mangano's Huggable Hanger, which was endorsed by Oprah Winfrey to create more organized, space-conserving closets, sold 300 million units and was HSN's top selling product of 2010 (Henry 2016).

Commitment to an idea, often through adversity, may look like the behavior of an idiot to many. But to innovators, it's natural. They have to commit because they can already see it working. They know there's something more, and they follow down that path.

Play is about doing. You jump in and try something and make a mess. You do stuff because it's fun, and it's all OK, because we're just playing around! And by that token, improv is about doing. You don't sit around, think through everything, and write a paper on an improv show. You get up on stage and do it. And you mess up, you start again, you're brilliant, you're awful, you fix stuff, you make things, and you learn things.

"Move fast and break things. Unless you are breaking stuff, you are not moving fast enough."

—Mark Zuckerberg

Researchers say that the most creative place in the world is in the shower. Our bodies and brains relax, the noise of the shower drowns out the outside world, and we breathe deeply. Great ideas come during that time. The second most creative place on earth is on vacation (Jacques 2014). No matter where it is, when we're on vacation, we're out of the normal curve of our lives—we're seeing and thinking about new things.

The behavior that sets creative thinkers and innovators apart is the propensity to do something about it. Most people have a great idea in the shower, get out, get dressed, go to work, and tell the story of their great idea a year later over cocktails. Innovators get out of the shower, dry off, and go do something about their idea.

After all, how did software engineer Lisa Seacat DeLuca come to have more than 100 patents? "The idea generation isn't the slow part," said DeLuca. "Anyone can come up with ideas very quickly. It's taking the time to write them down and do research to figure out if it's a great idea or how to make it an even better idea—that's really the bottleneck in innovation."

Case Study: Lightwell

Creative innovators do stuff and they often don't see it as creative. It's mostly problem solving in the moment. They run into roadblocks or frustrating issues that others simply accept, get annoyed because they can visualize a better way to do it, and make it happen to make their own lives easier.

Lightwell is a client of my company, ImprovEdge, and a woman-owned business in Dublin, Ohio; the United Kingdom; and Northern Ireland serving the tech industry. We worked with its leadership team to help them stay flexible, improvisational, and able to manage an extremely diverse employee base.

They have to manage well because they are driving a hotbed of innovation. "These are accidental innovations! I'm lucky enough to work with brilliant engineers who fix stuff just because they don't want to be bored," says Lightwell president Michelle Kerr, of the innovations the company keeps pumping out. "Although that sounds self-serving, it's how many of our breakthroughs occur. They're doing something they don't enjoy, so they find a way to change it, fix it, innovate it. It's such a part of their DNA; they usually forget to mention they've even done anything!"

Once Kerr was visiting the Belfast office and started chatting with an Italian engineer, Paul, who had transferred there. She asked him what he'd been up to, and after a shrug and "not much," he showed her a little process he had created for a new order management solution.

One of the worst parts of IT and development is testing. It's mundane, time-consuming, often faulty, and creates a bottleneck in getting new products to market. A lot of testing is outsourced to overseas companies. Paul was irritated with the whole process—he didn't want to spend the hundreds of hours it could take to do the test, and he didn't want to give up control and wait on an overseas firm to do the work. So, he created a sort of harness—a testing tool that pulled the work together and eliminated a huge amount of time and issues.

As Kerr took a closer look, she was astonished at the elegance and efficacy of his idea, and she realized this could be a product in and of itself. That led to bringing in the whole Belfast team, which dove in, assessing, brainstorming, testing, failing, and playing. They collaborated on a radical level to create a brand-new product for their clients using Paul's original idea as the springboard.

This "simple fix," as Paul first called it, takes the testing that used to require 2,000 hours and gets the same work done in 200 hours. Right now, a global retailer is considering using this product for order management across multiple continents.

I asked Kerr about her team and culture, because this is not the first time they've innovated on such an impressive scale. She responded that the propensity to find systemic solutions, rather than band-aids, seems to run through the team. They have an ingrained mantra—"Why not?"—which drives them to ask questions, talk to one another, and seek less-obvious opinions and outcomes. Ever since Lightwell's inception, Kerr and her team have created an environment of collaboration, questioning, and innovation. The awards crowded onto the shelves speak to the efficacy of this open, creative environment.

She also refuses to take any credit: "I'm an under-the-radar person. I may have identified the opportunity that Paul had uncovered, but it took the diversity of the team, and a lot of time and work and passion to bring this product to market."

Exercise: Story Game

Do you remember playing the telephone game as a kid? Someone started a short narrative, which was then sent around a circle, whispered from one ear to the next. The fun was in waiting to hear how the story changed by the time it reached the last ear. In this adult version, your group will have a chance to reconsider how they listen or don't listen, and how they adhere to a version or prefer to add their own details. It's best played with a group of 10 or more, and entertains your group while they sharpen their listening skills.

1. Each participant prepares a 30-second true story about themselves. It can be from today or years ago. It must be simple: "When I was 10, I played tag in the dark at summer camp. I tripped on a tent rope and broke my arm and the ambulance took an hour to arrive way out there!"

2. Ask everyone to pair up and share the story with a partner. Don't let on that there's more to come.

3. Now the listeners must retell the story they just heard—in first person, as if it was their own—to a new partner. They must tell the story exactly as they remember it, without even changing pronouns. (Which can be very funny when men have to retell stories of childbirth, for example.)

4. Repeat for one to two more rounds, each time retelling the story they just heard to a new partner. In this pattern, a participant will tell her own story, Tom's story, Jorge's story (which Jorge just heard from LaChandra), and Melissa's story (which has already gone through three other people).

5. After at least three rounds, ask several volunteers to tell the story they just heard. Then ask the real authors to identify themselves and tell the original version of their story. It may vary widely, with different names and details. Or it may not. It may be astonishingly close, even down to similar hand gestures.

6. Discuss as a group. What keeps us from really hearing a person's story? Why was a certain story easy to remember? How did it feel to have your story change so much? It may not be a big deal for a game, but what about information flowing at work? When the details really matter, we better be paying close attention!

Adventures With Innovation and Improvisation

We next meet our two heroes on the playing field. Innovation arrives first. She's riding a solar-powered scooter, and wearing a non-Newtonian smart material vest (to protect against impact in the game) and auto-lacing, custom 3-D printed athletic shoes. When she jumps down, she places her purse on a waterproof, collapsible chair she pulls out of her pocket.

Improvisation arrives just after, tumbling out of a pickup truck that's blaring music and filled with the most unusual assortment of people: musicians with their instruments, football players in full gear, a member of the U.S. Women's National Soccer team, a quadriplegic, four children at various stages of life, a large black Labrador, a cowboy, and a pregnant woman.

Thinking Upside Down

Improvisation grew out of the realization that theater and music could happen without a script or score. Actors realized that with collaboration, they did not have to be bound to the convention of another person's form or ideas. To further that concept, improvisers strive to use "the third idea." That means never going for the obvious—but instead using ideas or angles that no one expects. If the first thing that pops into your head is expected, the second thing will probably be more interesting. To push the envelope, improvisers strive to use the third idea, and not what the audience would expect. Reverse your assumptions and take the least-likely approach. Avoid hitting the audience over the head with the obvious. If they shout out "Potato chips!" as the suggestion for a scene, the last thing a good improviser would do is sit down and pantomime crunching on chips. Now if they suddenly start playing poker or chopping down a tree, there's a lot more room for something interesting to happen, and for potato chips to show up later in a completely surprising, and hopefully hilarious way.

One of the most impressive attributes of creative innovators is their ability to look at things differently. They think backward and upside down, often to amazing results. That tenacity to challenge the status quo, look beyond the obvious, and think differently is something that can be improved and learned over time. In this chapter, we'll explore a few aspects of thinking upside down that come directly from improvisation: thinking differently, justification, and creative constraint.

Thinking Differently

Thinking differently and challenging the status quo is one of the most important improvisational principles. One of my favorite examples of turning conventional thinking on its head is occurring not in a corporation or school, but in a prison in New Hampshire. The New Hampshire Department of Corrections has a mission statement, as do all state prison systems: "We treat all employees, offenders and the public with fairness, honesty, and dignity, while recognizing individual diversity." That sounds very promising, but our perception, and many of the news stories that come out of prison systems, certainly don't seem to be about dignity and fairness. But this prison system is different. It actually strives to reach its mission, and one county's prison system even achieves its goal.

Rick Van Wickler is the warden at Cheshire County Correctional Facility in New Hampshire. When he took over in 1993, the prison was bogged down in a massive corruption scandal that resulted in a murder-suicide committed by the last warden. Van Wickler spent the next 13 years visiting prisons around the country, picking and choosing components of the models he saw while also developing something completely new. He started to ask himself, what if we treat the prisoners like employees? What if we treat corrections officers as not just enforcers of the law, but as colleagues of the offenders? Van Wickler designed a different type of incarceration experience, and it has paid off.

Van Wickler's model altered the motto of the American Correctional Association, "Care, Custody, and Control," to "Care, Custody, and Management." When I interviewed Van Wickler, he talked about helping people change, by changing for them.

He also decided to put limits on the amount of punishment any one person would have to endure; even the highest level of confinement within his prison (lock down for 23 hours a day) comes with a time limit of 15 days.

Remember the discussion in chapter 2 about how to prepare the right environment for innovative success? This is exactly what Van Wickler did. First, the prison has no fences, no barbed wire. He wanted to integrate the prison into the community in the best way possible. In a 2014 interview with *Vice* magazine, Van Wickler explained, "Nobody wants a jail in their neighborhood, and we didn't want to make it obvious. Most people don't even know it's a jail. They think it's a school" (Morin 2014). He also wanted to alleviate the suffering of families and children who came to visit inmates, so the visitor lobby is bright and clean with inmate artwork hanging on the walls. Language plays another major role in creating a better environment. Inmates and officers refer to each other as "Ms." or "Mr." instead of "Inmate" and "Officer."

These foundational, up-front changes allowed Van Wickler to create a completely new atmosphere in the prison system, with lower rates of recidivism and violence. Van Wickler has also never had an escapee. He does his research: Inmates are classified by the type of crime they commit as well as their behavior reports. Each offender's level of freedom (while limited) is tailored to past behavior. This evaluation pays off in exponentially higher levels of compliance with rules and expectations.

The inmates are constantly supervised, but not through a double-sided mirror or a watchtower. Officers share space with the inmates and interact with them constantly, not just during inspections or roll call. Officers do bed and room checks, but when they "toss" a room (the act of completely taking a room apart to check for weapons, drugs, and so forth), they put it back the way they found it. The inmates note this as one of the most rare and surprising aspects of life in the facility. It fosters an environment of mutual respect that has a profound impact on the culture of the prison.

There's another reason why this culture of respect is so meaningful. Across the United States lack of respect in offices and warehouses results in lower retention rates and worse. Employees report higher numbers of sick days and lower job satisfaction when they do not feel respected (Prather n.d.). Management experts Christine Porath and Christine Pearson (2013) wrote in the *Harvard Business Review* that employees who are on the receiving end of incivility and disrespect report decreased quality of work, a decline in performance, and decrease in work effort. In a prison environment, lack of respect to prisoners can lead to violence not only against fellow inmates, but also against officers. The mutual environment of respect fostered in the Cheshire County Correctional Facility protects everyone and creates an environment of safety.

One inmate commented, "Here they're teaching us to be respectful of ourselves and one another, which of course, a lot of us need to learn." Mutual respect is so difficult in even the most ideal work environment, and Van Wickler is building a new type of incarceration program: one that results in less violence, fewer escapes, and a better working environment for prison employees. By turning every stereotype we have about prisons on its head, he's building a new way for every prison to reconsider incarceration.

Justification

In improv, we have a million ideas. When we get a suggestion from the audience, it can look like a Black Friday rush to the front of the stage there are so many ensemble members dying to leverage their ideas. Many times, two improvisers start doing something at the same time, even though they are not sure what the other might be doing. Two people, with two different ideas, suddenly find themselves in one scene together, and they have to make it work. Often, one of the actors will justify, or adjust, what they are doing.

Justification in improv is different than justification in life. When you justify something in life, it usually means you are proving a point, giving the motive or facts behind a situation to show why you are right or your actions were reasonable. In improv, it's all about making dichotomous situations work together. An improviser might be doing something, not knowing a totally different thing is going on at the other end of the stage, only to turn around and realize he suddenly has to make what he thought was rowing a boat look like sweeping a floor to make the scene work.

One of the most brilliant moments of justification I've seen was in a tiny show in a no-name black box theater in Chicago. The suggestion from the audience had been "construction." The first actor onstage chose the obvious and started applying mortar to bricks with a back and forth hand movement, as if he were using a trowel to slather on the mortar, then kept stacking the blocks. Unbeknownst to him, another ensemble member was doing the same back and forth hand movement next to him. He looked over at her, as she stacked her imaginary bricks together, then suddenly she took a big bite, taking her scene partner by surprise. She had been smoothing mayo on a sandwich, not stacking bricks!

He immediately justified the scene and his larger movements by asking to borrow her knife, using it to slather something on the top of his "wall," then picking up what we originally thought was a wall of bricks and taking a bite of his huge sandwich! The audience just went wild. Yet there was more to come. As they looked at each other, chewing their gigantic bites, the woman double-justified and said, "Nothing like a mortar in the morning!" So, although we thought it was only sandwiches, she let him justify her eating and she justified his concrete and bricks. Her scene partner immediately agreed and asked if he could pour her a nice cup of concrete. She accepted, and they went on to create a really funny scene about giants who ate bricks, mortar, concrete, tile flooring, and lumber, and saved sheetrock for dessert.

When innovators see something they did not expect and have to justify how it will work, they usually discover new possibilities. Have you ever played Pass the Pen? In that game, a common object is passed around a circle and everyone has to come up with a different use or explanation for the object. In the case of a common pen, it can be a pen, but it can also be a jar opener if you use it to wedge under the lid, or a tiny spear you throw, a little baton to twirl, a limbo stick for a Barbie doll, and on and on. The players keep justifying the object's many different possibilities.

Two examples from business history stand out as justifications: Avon and Wrigley. In both instances, the original founders set out to sell something completely different. In 1886 David H. McConnell set out to sell books door-to-door. However, because he usually spoke to a woman of the household, he began to offer small free bottles of perfume as an enticement. Those women became far more interested in the perfume than the books, and McConnell realized he needed to start selling more cosmetics. One remnant of McConnell's start is still evident, however; Avon is a global brand that built its success on door-to-door and in-home sales.

Not much later, William Wrigley Jr. tried to launch his baking powder and soap company. The freebie was a stick of gum. No one wanted the soap, but everyone wanted the gum.

You may think these are simple, obvious examples. But don't underestimate the tenacity of the mind. Two examples of innovations in the scientific world are practically the inverse of each other when we consider justification.

The first, anesthesia, reads like a centuries-old game of Pass the Pen. Performing surgery has always been a problem, due to the terrible pain and recovery it inflicts. But humankind also has a very long history of using substances recreationally for their drug-induced effects. So, ancient scientists began tinkering with drugs. The Sumerians used opium as a painkiller as far back as the third century B.C., the Chinese recorded intoxicating people to perform surgeries, and the use of inhaled narcotics can be traced back to the Persians.

Doctors and scientists were constantly trying to figure out how to deal with pain. But it was accidental observations and justifications that led to some of the most important outcomes in this arena. Believe it or not, there was an inhalant party culture in the Victorian era. In the 1800s, people were fully aware of the effects of ether and nitrous oxide—they made you feel drunk and funny, so they were used for "ether frolics" and "laughing parties." However, modern pain management was born when Horace Wells attended an exhibit in 1844 and saw a man injure his leg under the influence of laughing gas. The punch drunk subject reported he felt no pain, so Wells used the substance on himself to test the theory. In this case, the doctors followed the partiers and found a justification for the use of ether and nitrous oxide.

The reverse proved true for LSD. Swiss scientist Albert Hofmann spent many years experimenting with the capabilities of compounds derived from the fungus ergot. One compound was called LSD-25, and garnered little to no interest from the scientific community, so Hofmann shelved it for several years. When he took it out again, he accidentally ingested some of the compound. He began to feel strange, and during his bike ride home experienced wild and colorful visions. He had discovered one of the most powerful psychotropic drugs of our time, and the term *psychedelic* would forever mean kaleidoscope-like visions and experiences.

He wanted the drug to remain the territory of the medical psychiatric community. But, that sort of trip was not going to stay a secret. Where a scientist saw medical use, the populace justified another form of recreation. LSD became incredibly popular as a recreational drug in the 1960s. Hofmann hated that fact, and referred to the drug thereafter as his "problem child." This time the partiers followed the scientist, and justified his discovery as a mind-blowing new way to experience visions and the psychedelic landscape. That drug culture is credited with some of the most innovative music, literature, poetry, and art of the 20th century.

Justification, in the improvisational sense, is an innovative behavior. Something that looks wrong or off to the rest of the world, looks like something new to an innovator. What you intended to be one thing doesn't fit the current situation, so most people figure it can't work and throw it out the window. But innovators continue to ask, "How can this work?" or "How can I apply this differently?"

"I refuse to be intimidated by reality anymore. What is reality? Nothing but a collective hunch."

—Lily Tomlin

Creative Constraint

Where do great ideas come from? Many of us imagine creativity comes from an environment of boundless possibility—no rules or restrictions. We also have a stereotype of "creatives"—they work in cool studios rather than office buildings, wear jeans instead of suits, play table tennis most of the day, and are filled with endless creative solutions. And yes, there is a section in this book on the importance of environment and how openness can influence creativity. But remember our initial argument about innovation? It has dichotomous aspects, as does creativity.

Why should creativity be the province of a totally open environment or a certain type of person? We falsely think that if our world or profession is constrained, we cannot enjoy wild creativity. That just isn't the case. There are many benefits to boundaries when working creatively, and honestly, so many innovations came about because of boundaries.

Something couldn't be done a certain way due to boundaries, so an innovator came up with a creative solution.

It sounds counterintuitive, but boundaries can actually boost creativity. Think about procrastination—deadlines are often the single factor that ensures projects get done. As Dave Gray (2005), author and blogger, commented, "Creativity is driven by constraints. When we have limited resources—even when the limits are artificial—creative thinking is enhanced. That's because the fewer resources you have, the more you are forced to rely on your ingenuity."

When there are no boundaries, the possibilities may seem too large. Almost everyone has been faced with the terror of the endless blank page when writer's block sets in, or a project with no clear scope and no idea where to start. When there are no boundaries, the possibilities may seem too large. Boundaries don't simply provide swim lanes for definition; they create issues that must be overcome. Puzzles challenge the mind and when constraints create blockades, the brain kicks into overdrive.

That's why some of the greatest art and innovation has come from a situation of constraint. The fewer resources you have, the more you must rely on your ingenuity—creative thinking is enhanced when all the obvious options are off the table. As author and strategist Adam Richardson (2013) discussed in the *Harvard Business Review*, "Constraints have a Goldilocks quality: too many and you will indeed suffocate in stale thinking, too few and you risk a rambling vision quest. The key to spurring creativity isn't the removal of all constraints . . . you should impose those constraints that move you toward clarity of purpose."

One incredible example of the tenacity to keep trying options in an extreme environment of constraint happened in 1970 during the Apollo 13 lunar mission. The launch was successful, but a fault from inside the space module caused an explosion that turned the exploration into a test for survival for the crew. Due to damage caused by the explosion, the astronauts were forced to stay in the lunar module. However, the lunar module wasn't built to house that many men, and the carbon dioxide they exhaled began to build up in the module. On the ground, an engineering team had to figure out a way to clean the air with only the equipment on board and very little time. It was the unbelievable constraints and the pressure of lives at risk that drove them to a totally unexpected solution.

They figured out a way for the command module's square air cleaners to be used in the lunar module's round receivers. Who says a square peg can't fit in a round hole?

Improvisation provides a perfect template for constrained creativity. Improvisational performers have none of the common tools of theater—such as a script, props, or costumes—that would be the open and unedited side of the equation. The blank stage is the blank canvas. However, improvisers also have to follow important rules: Every contribution must be accepted and used, you cannot deny anything that happens onstage, and you must integrate and acknowledge the contributions of the audience (which are often difficult and contradictory). While "improv" seems to imply the absence of constraints, most scenes are based around suggestions from the audience. This is what makes improv so enjoyable and creative. Yet within all these constraints, improvisers find the most creative outcomes. Improvisational performers see the dearth of resources as a golden opportunity rather than a problem. By adhering to these boundaries, improvisers know they can be wildly creative in other ways.

As a matter of fact, many professions that are seen from the outside as extremely constrained are peopled by the highly creative. Attorneys and software developers work within extreme boundaries and the most successful are often those who are most creative despite the limitations of their fields.

So how does this apply to you, your work, and your efforts to learn more innovative behaviors? Here's one example: My company was once tasked to stretch the thinking, strategy, and creativity of the distribution leadership team of one of the largest retailers in the United States. We found that the executives were often lazy in their brainstorming. This was around 2003-2004, and they had gigantic budgets, huge numbers of employees, and seemingly endless resources. You would think that with that surplus, anything would be possible. On the contrary, they seemed to care very little for innovation because the entire enterprise was fat and happy.

In our practice exercises, we imposed ridiculous boundaries of time and money and demanded high-level outcomes. We called it the Ultimate Challenge. For example, we asked them to light an entire warehouse with only one light bulb, $5 for supplies, and two hours of work. Or we asked them to take a high school juvenile delinquent and make her able to run a new division of their company in 48 hours or less, with a $100 budget. I finally saw them lean in, work hard, and come up with a few startling ideas—but only because they were forced to.

When constraint becomes mandatory, we suddenly have to recalibrate how we work. The economic downturn in 2008 forced us to realize that business will never, ever be conducted in the same way again. We must be more innovative, leaner, faster, and smarter. Companies have started collaborating with former competitors, building unforeseen relationships with their clients through social media, and creating products that are better, yet cheaper. They've discovered creative ways to address unexpected constraints.

I've used the Ultimate Challenge many times with lower level and far more creative teams than the C-level executives in 2004. One of my favorite solutions ever came from a group in a healthcare company. When faced with the challenge to light the warehouse with so few resources, they took me at my word. They used their $5 to buy a box of matches and set the warehouse on fire. When I laughed in delight and surprise at their solution, they simply fired back, "You told us to light it!"

Rather than being frustrated by compliance, legal, or financial issues, embrace them. Ask the people who impose the boundaries to join your next brainstorming session—what new ideas do they have?

When a situation seems too hard, too locked down, and surrounded by boundaries, think like an improviser. At the same time, be open to boundless possibility. Sounds like a dichotomy? It is; that's why truly innovative individuals, teams, and organizations are so flexible. They sense the tension and embrace it. They try different tactics, invite open-minded thinkers, and see boundaries as creative catalysts. And oh yes, they improvise.

Combining Thinking Upside Down, Justification, and Creative Constraint

In many of the stories and examples in this book, we discussed outliers; people, teams, and organizations who went against the status quo, saw things differently, and innovated. The question for the future is, "Why are they unusual?"

Why can't innovative and collaborative behaviors be more common? There are myriad reasons why society, education, religion, and hierarchy lock us down. But those realities are changing, albeit slowly. The future could be one in which our behaviors are radically different, and our rate of innovation accelerates exponentially. The Hole in the Wall Project is one example where that exponential innovation is happening.

Sugata Mitra, professor of educational technology at Newcastle University, decided to think upside down and conduct a radical experiment. Up to this point, education has been based on a rote memory and "tell to teach" model originating around the Victorian British Empire—teach thousands of people to learn specific skills and repeat them without question.

In 1999, he placed a working, connected, English-language computer in a slum in India; one of the most constrained places on earth, where education and literacy rates are very low and every person lives in poverty. It was installed low to the ground, so that children could see and access it. He told the children it was a computer and without further information, left. He never explained or taught them anything, so they had to justify the appearance of something new in their world. What was it, and how could they use it?

The children's natural curiosity took over, and when Mitra and a colleague returned eight hours later, the children were browsing the Internet. That seemed impossible, so the colleague suggested that a programmer from the nearby computer school had taught the children to browse. Mitra wanted to find out. He went 300 miles away to a remote, poverty-stricken village where there was no English and installed another English-language computer in the same way. When Mitra returned two months later, he was astounded; the children had taught themselves English, used the computer daily, and asked for "a faster processor and a better mouse."

He expanded his experiment by placing computers in remote villages where there was zero computer literacy or English, and added another wrinkle. He wanted to make success an impossibility and disprove his own experiment. He loaded a computer with college-level information about the biotechnology of DNA in English, and asked the children to learn it.

When he returned two months later, the six- to 12-year-old children in the village had gone from a 0 percent understanding of DNA biology to a 30 percent understanding of college-level concepts. As of 2015, Mitra's experiments in education have expanded to schools all over the globe. His data have determined that children, when left alone with a computer and one another, can reach the same standard of language and computer usage as a Western secretary in nine months.

And he keeps thinking upside down! His most recent wrinkle in the experiment is the "granny cloud." Teachers, grandmothers, and other volunteers connect virtually with children in villages across the world to offer encouragement. They don't teach or tell, instead they ask questions, compliment the children on their smarts, stand back, and watch with awe and encouragement. That additional level of support made the children's achievements spike exponentially.

Isn't that the definition of improvisation? We supply a compelling idea or question, give it to a group that is collaborative and playful, and stand back, applaud, and watch what is created with amazement. It is exactly like the collaborative, improvisational nature of the children who access the computers. This incredible innovation in education is changing the way these children behave—not only toward one another, but also toward the world.

Mitra envisions a future where classrooms are collaborative spaces and tests are experiences where groups of kids interact with one another and their resources, both online and off, to come up with interesting answers to problems. He sees education being a mix of interaction and encouragement, group exploration, and self-driven curiosity.

If we are going to truly innovate, it is our responsibility to look around at our world. What institutions and expectations are we preserving that are smacking the creativity out of the next generation? We must prepare a better environment, say "yes, and," think upside down, and play. Our future depends on it.

Case Study: LWOW (Law Without Walls)

Michele DeStefano was frustrated. Her work as a legal professor at University of Miami and affiliated faculty at Harvard Law School's Center on the Legal Profession demanded that she prepare her students and retrain practicing lawyers for a changing world of global issues and technology. She knew law students and lawyers needed to be able to collaborate, innovate, and improvise in a world of constantly changing legal realities. The problem was that traditional in-person law school or CLE (continuing legal education) did nothing to develop the collaborative skills needed by the lawyers of the future. Current legal education, and legal practice for that matter, stymies creative and collaborative behaviors. They are ridden with hierarchies (based on rank, expertise, and title), barriers to entry, and staid ways of training and learning. Think of some of the worst stereotypes of the legal industry today: They are rigidly hierarchical, risk-averse to a fault, noninclusive, and competitive to a point that shuts down collaboration even within the same firm.

"I was looking everywhere for options for my students," DeStefano recalls. "At first, I tried to expand their perspective from within traditional courses to show them a different way to work. But that didn't do it. As I slowly found like-minded people, who were not always attorneys, it struck me: I could build a completely different approach to how we train and upskill lawyers and how we change the future of the legal industry."

The legal industry needs to improvise!

There was no question in DeStefano's mind that 21st-century attorneys would require a completely new and fresh approach to training, innovating, and community building. She began to think upside down and saw an approach that was utterly counterintuitive to the protective, risk-averse culture of the legal industry. Constraints are everywhere in the law, but this only inspired DeStefano. "Sometimes, when I started to explain my ideas, people would just shut me down," she explained. "I kept hearing, 'But that won't work for our firm,' or 'That's not how legal education is supposed to work,' but for every one of those, I began to find people who were as frustrated as I was and really excited about this opportunity."

The first time I spoke to DeStefano in early 2013, she had already built the foundation of LawWithoutWalls (LWOW), an interdisciplinary teaming community to explore and solve the biggest problems in global law today, and train 21st-century skills in the process. "I think lawyers need to be out of their comfort zone—we need to understand how to improvise," she laughed over the phone. "And not be terrified of the idea!"

My company collaborated with LWOW to bring the behaviors and messages of improvisation to this cutting-edge venture. One of the main reasons we collaborated to bring improv to the LWOW culture was because DeStefano didn't stop with attorneys. True to form, she wanted the experience to be more than training or mentoring. Because so much of the legal industry is about looking backward, she wanted to think upside down and look forward. In addition to attorneys, law students, and law professors, she partnered with technologists, venture capitalists, and business executives. We worked with this diverse group to help them institute the behaviors of improvisation. They practiced saying "yes, and," preparing a positive environment, playing, focusing, and thinking upside down.

This set of behaviors was critical because LWOW participants have to create a project of worth, which is the focus of a four-month collaborative project. Every year in January, law students, professors, attorneys, legal entrepreneurs, legal service providers, technologists, venture capitalists, and a diverse collection of interested people converge to discuss issues, build teams in person, and participate in a mini-hackathon. (To borrow a term from computer programming, a *hackathon* is an event where many participants gather to do collaborative programming.) After this kickoff, the teams spend the next four months interacting virtually across the globe to solve a substantive legal issue—a project of worth. That's the point of all the teaming and collaborating and moving outside one's comfort zone. It's to be equipped to solve all the issues that are keeping the legal industry in a state of stress and decay!

The virtual work is fantastic. Once the groups identify their projects, they begin collaborating every week. A law student in China will videoconference with her team, which consists of a lawyer in England, a professor in the United States, perhaps three other students in South America, and a technologist in Germany. In addition, DeStefano hosts a virtual classroom every week featuring technologists serving the legal industry, or futurists who are writing about the next century, or a venture capitalist who understands what works and what doesn't in business. The platform allows everyone to interact in real time with audio and video, see the speakers, come on camera to ask questions, post articles for reference, and so much more. The walls of distance, region, and language are torn down so that these unexpected groups can improvise together.

In April, everyone reconvenes at ConPosium. The students, along with two mentors (the team leaders), present their solutions, receive suggestions and feedback, and have the opportunity to grow professionally, personally, and intellectually. And sometimes, their solutions are so interesting, they receive funding from the technology and venture capitalists who also attend the meeting.

For example, Advocat was an idea born of the issues lawyers deal with in attempting to protect and represent their minor clients during immigration trials. Minors are often deported by choice because they are scared and alone and do not trust the system. The technology in Advocat is a revolutionary, multilingual interface for minor immigrant detainees and their advocates, which uses gamification to build trust and explain and safeguard the best interests of the child. It helps the children understand what is happening, and gives their advocates the best information to represent them.

"I couldn't believe the support and excitement that poured out for our project," said one of the students involved in the project. "I learned more in four months than I have throughout my entire law school experience, and I feel like I'm making a difference. This legal issue, for vulnerable minors, made me anxious and frustrated. And we're already seeing positive outcomes; it's been incredible."

WhiteHatters (now incorporated under Fissure Security Limited) increases cybersecurity protection and builds awareness against targeted phishing attacks through simulation and deconstruction learning. From their partnership at ConPosium, they are currently meeting with multiple law firms who are beginning to beta test their product.

Enterprises, law firms, and universities such as Lockheed Martin, Microsoft, Spotify, Bupa, Ricoh, Barclays, Harvard Law School, University of St. Gallen, IE University, Legal Zoom, Eversheds, Pinsent Masons, and

King & Wood Mallesons have sponsored LWOW. And some have hired Michele and her team to lead internal programs based on the LWOW model to create learning and teaming projects for their employees.

As exciting as ConPosium can be, DeStefano is quick to remind people, "Although a few projects have been brought to market and LWOW has inspired some participants to become startups, the real value (and mission of) LWOW is to change mindsets and behavior. Over time, the experience of leading a global team in a project of worth helps these legal professionals and students to hone the skills of future leaders and complex collaborative problem solvers. LWOW creates a vehicle to connect those interested in changing the law market to work together to solve real issues through technology, collaboration, innovation, and improvisation."

Exercise: T.A.G. (The Acronym Game)

Get your team engaged and out of its normal work frame of mind. Let individuals discover how critical it is to use their own strengths to help their teams. This activity moves participants from relying solely on themselves to relying on their teams. Words fly back and forth, the challenge becomes more difficult, and teams realize they can't go it alone.

1. Arrange your group into two or more teams. Give each group paper and a pencil, and have them nominate a scribe.

2. Have the group choose a three-letter word; for example, dog

3. Each team has two minutes to come up with as many different phrases or sentences following the letters in the word.

   ° Example: Denise Owns Gardens. Dragons Only Growl. Don't Out Grow.

4. Repeat words are NOT allowed.

   ° Example: Dragons Only Growl. Dragons Only Grow. Dragons Only Grump.

   ° Only one of those sentences counts. The phrases must make sense.

5. Let the teams work for two minutes, then count their phrases to determine the winner of the first round.

6. Ask them how they worked. Very often, you'll hear that one person did all the writing, several people came up with phrases, and

sometimes a person or two didn't participate at all. Sometimes they laugh and say something like, "Samia did all the work! I just had to offer support." Invariably, individuals usually contribute entire three-word phrases.

7. Second Round: Use a five-letter word. You'll see a bit more collaboration on this one, and the list may be shorter.

8. Third Round: Use an unexpectedly long word, like your company name. Especially if it's Nationally Recognized Engineers. Remind the teams that every entry has to make sense as a sentence or phrase.

You'll find that people can work alone on the short words. As they get longer, the whole team pitches in, trying to build cohesive sentences in two minutes. Greater challenge demands greater involvement. When the going gets tough, you need your team.

Adventures With Innovation and Improvisation

It's a Wednesday afternoon and Improvisation looks out at the city below from the 30th floor of the FlipPhysics headquarters. He nervously adjusts his tie, thinking that while he's never worn one before, he really liked the feeling of strength he got when he'd looked in the mirror that morning. When Innovation walks in the room, he gasps with surprise at her hiking boots, messy hair, and huge smile. They've been planning this day for months but he still can't believe it is happening. He and Innovation are about to make a big announcement.

You ready for this?

Ready. But this is going to be a really interesting day. Hope they don't all freak out.

They walk down to the large conference room together where the video cameras are on and the entire global population of FlipPhysics is gathered.

The tech pro comes up and starts pinning the mic onto Innovation's collar. She shakes her head and points to Improvisation. The tech gives a startled look, shrugs, and pins the mic onto Improv.

I almost didn't recognize you, Improv.

Hey everybody! I'm happy to announce that Innovation is heading out for a new adventure.

She's going to be fulfilling the role of Improvisation for the next two years. She'll be stepping out onto a limb and doing some really unexpected stuff.

During her travels, I'll be helping to fulfill the role of Innovation. We're excited and a little scared to reverse roles. So I'll need help! Let me know if you'd like to join the leadership team.

Inno steps up, throws a bucket of candy and soft toys at the crowd, and walks out the door.

Have fun!

Improv is relieved to see colleagues making their way up to talk to him.

Final Thoughts
Managing Change
Through Improvisation

The whole world is changing under our feet. As we walk toward the future, we don't know what's going to happen next or what direction our path will take. Change can create equal parts fear, anticipation, and stomach pain.

We resist change because of our ingrained patterns and the constant pressure of life; we want to do things the way we know because we're pressured for time. We want to save face because we don't want to look stupid in front of colleagues. We want to protect our source of income, and we fear the unknown. This is very messy stuff.

Harvard Business School professor Michael Tushman extolled the importance of not getting locked into the past in his work on dissent. "The key," he said, "is to hold paradoxical ideas . . . to think in the future and the past, simultaneously. . . . People prefer not to know about the future because it's so threatening to entrenched interests and to career competencies."

Innovations often lead to very difficult change; people are losing their jobs and processes and products are increasingly obsolete. It is absolutely possible that we will, if we haven't already, suffer mightily from innovation and change. Most of the stories I've told previously were about how people leaned into change, improvised, and benefitted. But there have been many times in my life where change was difficult, emotional, and life-changing in a painful way.

All the more reason to be an improviser. These behaviors travel across industries and will stand you in good stead no matter what happens. The key is to be aware of your options. Let's look at three final topics that will allow you to better manage the inevitable change that comes along with innovation. Let's explore connections, brain science, and letting go of control.

Connections, Trust, and Better Outcomes

When things go haywire, the first thing we do is look around for someone we trust. Imagine that you walk into work and there's an unexpected announcement that your office is closing, a buyout is taking place, a leader has suddenly stepped down, or the company has lost a major client. Trust equals safety, and when our fear and worry kicks in due to change we run to someone safe. We want to discuss our surprise and concern with someone to whom we are connected, who has been there before, who has our back. The important part is to create those connections before the crisis.

Granted, crisis is often the driver of sudden, deep connections. We all know the stories of people who've formed lifelong bonds over the shared experience of crisis. However, crisis in corporate environments can sometimes be a drawn-out affair. It's not as though we can pull together for a day and solve everything.

So, spend some time thinking about your connections. There are two levels you can consider: First, how close are you to the closest people? Have you taken the time to really get to know your colleagues, team, and even vendors you work with? Is it always "work as usual" or have you strengthened those relationships through conversation and collaboration? Consider your obvious relationships of family, neighborhood, place of worship, or school; the people who are part of the constant fabric of your life may have so much more to offer if you get to know them better.

Second, improvisation encourages diversity, but getting to know people who are very different from us can be uncomfortable. That's OK! As long as you approach conversations and interactions with good intentions and a dose of humility, it will be worth it. We all trip up, and it takes some time to get to know people who are different. If you make a mistake, apologize, (hopefully) laugh together, and try again. Most important, don't hesitate—take the time to speak with, get to know, and engage with people; find commonalities. Even the smallest, seemingly inconsequential connections can have impressive results.

Alex Pentland, author of *Social Physics* and an MIT computer scientist researching big data, did a study on the power of small connections. He was most interested in human, face-to-face interactions, so he and his team looked for an environment in need of change. They chose to work with a banking call center that had certain individuals and teams suffering from poor performance. Call centers are a great environment for research because everything is measured: the amount of time to pick up a call, amount of time with the client, words used by both the client and the call center pro, and exact results and outcomes. The researchers persuaded the call center leadership to allow the whole team to take their coffee break together. This is normally restricted, because a call center always needs staff covering the lines, but leadership was so desperate that they were willing to try anything.

The group coffee break was the only major change that constituted the study. I know you're waiting for me to tell you about the special programming or intensive coaching that happened during those breaks. But Pentland and his associates didn't know or control what the team talked about; all we can assume was that the team took time together, socialized, commiserated on issues, connected with ideas, and got to know one another. Face-to-face.

That was the crux of his research—what is the impact of face-to-face interactions? Rather than working the phone lines and taking solitary breaks, the team was able to have daily human, face-to-face connection time. The results in increased speed and efficacy were dramatic. I'm sure bank leadership must have been dumbfounded when they saw the results.

Once it was clear that human connections were clearly positively affecting sales, the bank instituted this practice throughout its call centers, and generated an additional $15 million in revenue.

The smallest connections matter. Don't discount the power of knowing your colleague's favorite coffee drink or pet's name. Those are the building blocks of trust.

Change, the Brain, and Dealing With Tough Moments

One of the most important things to realize about change is that it messes with your brain. Stress and change affect the flow of hormones and chemicals that guide your brain function and can have serious implications. David Rock and Jeffrey Schwartz have conducted fascinating experiments on the effects of change and difficulty on the human brain, and how that is connected to organizational success or failure.

One of the most problematic effects of change is that when things don't match up, and are unexpected, the brain sends out an error message. Warning: Things are not correct from a cognitive standpoint. When that happens, our frontal lobes—which are responsible for logical, rational, higher-level function—are besieged by hormones, such as cortisol, that our ancient brain releases. Those chemicals are responsible for our more instinctual behaviors, such as fight, flight, or freeze.

To simulate these experiences for our clients we created an exercise called Hands Up, Stand Up!, which teaches three or four very simple activities cued by nonrelational words. For example, when I say, "Hands up," I am actually telling my audience to stand up. When I say, "Sit down," I'm telling them to put their hands up. They often giggle nervously as I teach them the different aspects of the game. When we practice as a group, they are often completely successful.

However, when the game begins I randomize the instructions and speed up the pace. Suddenly, the group is trying to translate the instructions, match them with unrelated activities, and keep up with a much faster pace. They are having to learn, implement, change, and improvise all at once. The game is very disconcerting by design. Some people are focused and have an intense look of concentration; they usually report feeling angry or drained afterward. Some people become so confused they can't think straight, so they sit down with a laugh and bail out. Others lose their place, try to jump back in, or watch another person to get back on track. Of course, watching another person who is also floundering doesn't work.

The point is that there are many different, extreme, and funny responses to this difficult experience. And those responses to the game are the same that often happen during change in an organization. Consider the strange behaviors of people during a major organizational change, such as a merger. People are being asked to do things they've never done—sometimes their instructions are in direct conflict with the ways they are used to doing things, they are struggling with fear, and the pace of events has accelerated. Their brains are dealing with a daily dose of stress hormones. Like the game players, they bail out by quitting their jobs, try to force control through concentration and anger, and emulate others around them, which may lead to multiple people engaging in bad behavior.

We must realize that change can lead to some freak-outs.

The question is, how do we deal with it? We breathe, observe, and ask questions.

The first, most effective step is to breathe. Remember our discussion about focus in chapter 3? Disorientation and wild behavior often come about because we are multitasking and trying to manage stress at the same time. When that occurs, we stop breathing deeply. We hold our breath (often unconsciously), slump (which forces our breath to become very shallow), and tighten our neck and shoulder muscles. These responses cut off the oxygen to our brain, which in turn, makes us more stressed.

Performers have known this for centuries! We get nervous and scared before every show, so we have a process to take care of this. Have you ever the seen funny scenes onstage or in the movies of actors or singers warming up? People love to lampoon the ridiculous breath, mouth, and body exercises we go through to get ready for the stage, and I will admit, they are goofy. But they work.

Now don't get worried. I'm not going to ask you to do a tongue-twister and deep knee bends in the middle of the office. But I am asking you to reevaluate how you manage your oxygen. Do you stretch or breathe deeply at home every day before work? If not, you are heading out onto your own stage unprepared. When we work with professionals who negotiate deals, we teach them breathing techniques they can use in the car or before a meeting, and even really sneaky ones they can use right in front of another person and they'll never know. You need ways to calm your nervous system and get grounded.

So, find a breathing technique! I don't care which one it is; you can use yoga techniques, search the Internet, or make one up on your own. I also highly recommend any singing class or choir. Just understand that you need a technique in your pocket to use during stressful moments. Breathe, calm down, and you'll have a clearer head.

Next is observation. On the improv stage, we are in a heightened state of observation because we rarely get a clear explanation of the activities going on around us. Our troupe member is engaged in a silent activity and we must figure out what they're doing before we can jump in. If you are in the middle of a scene and someone walks over with a strange gait and look on his face, you'll have to gauge how to react.

During change, it's easy to hole up or become myopic. This is the time to look around, not only at your environment and companions, but also at anything else that can inform you. Keep an eye on the media, industry, government, or culture around you. Look for the unexpected next to the familiar; if something seems unusual, watch it for a while. Why is it happening? The more you know and understand, the better choices you'll be able to make.

Finally, ask questions. It seems so obvious, yet our need to shore up our ego may keep us from speaking up for fear of looking dumb. Or we may not want to draw attention to ourselves. But how will we truly know if we don't understand? Open-ended questions are the secret to managing life's challenges because they demand long, narrative answers, rather than a simple yes or no.

For example, if you are in a tough negotiation or confusing situation with your team, ask an open-ended question. This gets other people talking, so you'll learn a lot and get a chance to breathe and think all at once. This technique can even help you save face. If someone fires a tough question at you, it's not necessary to answer right away. Instead say, "That's interesting. Could you tell me more about your view on that?"

It's disarming; they'll start expounding, which gives you more time to think about your response.

Collaboration Is Stronger Than Control

One of the first things we do when we sense change is clamp down; we believe that by strong-arming a situation, we can maintain control, get what we want, and force the change into submission. And sometimes that's successful. We do get our way, and it seems that if we continue to be tough, we'll always be able to stem the tide of change and keep control. But as history will prove a million times over, change will not be kept locked in a box. Sometimes you must let go and see what happens.

The key is that when you let go, you don't do it alone. To get through change, even when it's scary, we must collaborate with others. Improvisers work with their troupes to get through times of uncertainty. They are never alone, so giving up control and facing the future becomes a group experience. The first thing to ask yourself is, "Who's in my troupe? Who has my back?"

There's a great improvisational game called Time Dash. In the game, the first two volunteers are asked to choose a moment in time around a major life event (like a baby's birth or a car accident) and play out a scene. For example, if the event is a wedding, one volunteer might say, "Six months before!" at which point she'll bump into her partner onstage, fall over as if she's spilled a huge bag of groceries, look up, and go googly eyed. We can all see that through this crazy moment of accidentally bumping into a person, she's trying to set up a story about how they met. And if her partner is staying flexible, he or she will play the scene, also falling and looking struck by her—literally falling in love at first sight.

But Time Dash can't be about one moment in time. Even if those first two were successful and got a laugh, they must give up the stage to another member of the troupe who chooses a different moment.

This game can be fantastic, but I've also seen it fall apart. As with the concept of "scriptwriting," failure in Time Dash comes when someone wants to control the game. Somebody will decide that he has a great idea for the story and doesn't like the fact that someone else messed with his preconceived notion. So, he'll step out and "tell" rather than collaborate.

In improv, "telling" happens when a player steps out as a self-appointed narrator and lays out the facts, characters, and plot lines for the audience. It can be a very effective device, but not when someone uses it to squash other storylines. By denying other contributions, telling the audience (and therefore the troupe onstage) what they are supposed to know and do, she forces a kind of hierarchical control. Let me tell you from experience, it annoys the troupe, confuses the audience, and usually smashes the laughs. The worst part is that it is so obvious; even the most novice audience member has commented to me, "What was that when she stepped out and told everyone what to do? That was so weird, and didn't follow the story onstage."

Some readers must be thinking, "That's great. But how do you change a hierarchical, controlling organization?! That's crazy-talk. . . ."

It's possible! My company once worked with a large pharmaceutical and biotechnology company that was struggling with change. They were in the difficult process of acquiring multiple companies, developing and distributing new drugs, and opening new markets. Their core business had been around for many decades, and up to this point had functioned very well using a hierarchical command and control kind of management model.

Whether they were scientists, factory workers, salespeople, or part of management, if people entered the company in junior status, worked hard, and did what they were told, they were often able to have nice, long careers at one place. But we all know how that story ends. Suddenly, everything was changing. Scientists learned that the research they started five years earlier was no longer part of the strategy and the funding was going away. Factory and distribution workers learned that previous timeframes, resources, and processes were all under review, and starting to change. Salespeople had to move their families to new territories with no guarantees, and executives were trying to deal with new pressure from the market and shareholders.

Brains were under siege and people were having all sorts of wild, emotional reactions. There was a constant refrain echoing through the halls of senior management, "I told them to do it, but they didn't!" And employees were saying, "I can't do that because it's impossible!" Everybody was frustrated.

We developed a five-part series to teach improvisational behaviors and make collaboration an intrinsic part of the culture. The first step was rolling out a full-day workshop called Managing Tough Conversations. The crux of the issue was that culturally, when things were rough, management had fallen back to the old ways of telling and then expecting people to follow instructions without comment. Because of all the change, especially the integration of new cultures from acquired companies, that mode of leadership was never going to work again.

In the workshop we divided the senior management team, which was composed of more than 350 people, into groups of 30. The groups were always a mix of executives, distribution center leaders, science leaders, and sales leaders. Those workshops were intense! The leaders were so used to total control that we first had to prove the higher efficacy of collaboration and how it could make their lives easier. You see, the irony of giving up control is that it allows others to come up with solutions, which makes them feel ownership because they are involved. Having skin in the game inspires them to work harder to make sure their process or solution is a success. Although it can be scary to give up control, we practiced using role play and then applied those lessons to real situations that were happening back at the office or facility.

The senior managers also learned key communication techniques, such as reflections, open-ended questions, and straightforward opening statements. They learned that there's no hiding behind euphemisms. We worked on observing situations before making snap decisions, and breathing to keep clarity. They also learned, role played, and practiced a three-step process for collaboratively, positively managing any tough situation that could occur.

And boy were there some doozies! One manager told us, "Thanks to this process, I've been able to literally save my team. Before the workshop, I was on the brink of firing 50 percent of my people—we didn't understand each other at all and were constantly at odds. Once I gave them the trust and room to be part of the solution, everything turned around. I feel responsible for some of the initial problems, but now feel really proud of the turnaround—we did it all together, and my team came up with most of the creative solutions."

The leadership had to implement the process right away. Part two occurred 60 days after the workshop, when we held a virtual reunion through a videoconference to hear about their successes and concerns. We all responded, gave suggestions, and included email follow-up of one-on-one coaching or curated resource materials. One leader said, "I didn't realize how much I would need the videoconference. I'd been integrating the process, but hearing about my cohorts' struggles helped me realize that change is hard! That videoconference allowed me to give myself a pat on the back, and realized I was making progress."

Right after the videoconference, step three was making an internal cohort. One of the leaders would agree to keep the learning going, and the entire group would commit to connecting internally to support, learn from, and advise one another every month. We reminded them that the key was to keep one another honest; when someone was falling back into "control" mode, the group's job was to help them devise a way to reenter "collaborate" mode. The outcomes from this connection time were surprising new innovations.

For example, one sales leader told us, "We're all so busy, I didn't think I had the time to get to know our manufacturing supervisor. But the forced cohort time made me realize we had a lot in common. So I went to visit the plant and realized we've been telling the story of our product all wrong! There's huge benefit to our customers in the way we manufacture—it's transformed our conversations in the field, and sales have blossomed."

Step four was an evaluation four months after the workshop. Workshop participants evaluated themselves, and their peers, managers, and employees also rated them on how well they were integrating collaboration into everyday life at the company. One employee commented in the online survey, "I'm really glad you cared enough to ask me about my opinion. My manager shared this process with us, and I've been impressed with how much she is working to improve. Understanding what the company is doing has helped me be a better employee. I feel hopeful again."

Finally, we rolled out an e-learning version of Managing Tough Conversations. Now, thousands of employees could benefit from understanding how the process could help them collaborate with their managers and peers. The program integrated lessons from improv and humor to help drive the lessons of collaboration, and make a serious topic easier to digest.

In the midst of massive change, everyone was learning to improvise. One of the best outcomes of the experience was a calmer approach to reality. There were some people who didn't change because they believed the upset was temporary, and that everything would go back to "normal" once it slowed down. But as one employee noted after watching the e-learning program, "I feel as though I have techniques to handle my work conversations now. I thought this might all go away eventually, but my manager has helped me realize that this constant change is how we are going to function. It's the way we are going to grow, and improve. So I have to grow and improve right along with it."

Go With It

You have the ability to transform, change, and create in ways we can't even predict. And yes, fear, failure, uncertainty, and discomfort are part of the package. But you're an improviser. You will prepare, play, and think upside down, and you won't be alone. Your troupe, which will be changing constantly, will be along for the ride. So get up on your stage, look around, and improvise.

Acknowledgments

So many people supported the creation of this book. First, thanks to my wonderful family: my husband, Todd Majidzadeh (who continues to love and encourage me despite my going back for a third helping of crazy); my kids, Timothy, Kate, and Trey; my parents, David and Cathy Hough and Mary Lee and Tom Hedrick; and my many dear cousins across the country!

The incredible, improvisational ImprovEdge Ensemble: Melissa Smolko (who runs this place), April Olt, Christy Fryman, Jason Sudy, Dionysia Williams, Erika Jackson, David Thompson, Brooke Cartus, Mike Everett-Lane, Jamie Pachino, Michael Shepperd, Michelle Wilson, Sonda Staley, Dan Montour, Christy Wurdack, and Randy Carr.

The ATD team was fantastic: Tim Ito, Ann Parker, Clara Von Ins, Kathryn Stafford (whose steady hand kept me focused), Melissa Jones, Caroline Coppel, Julia Liapidova, Fran Fernandez, and Iris Sanchez. In addition, thanks to Ron Lippock who originally encouraged me to take my research and ideas and make them into a book.

Thanks to my clients and case study partners who were featured in the book: Ann Arvia, Michele DeStefano, Kurt Tunnell, Marty Vian, Michelle Kerr, Dan Creekmur, Terence Morley, Liz Moran, Ben Verwer, LaChandra Baker, and Alan Robinson.

Thanks to Julia Biesenthal of Flight Media for designing the change model.

Acknowledgments

My improv training, inspiration, performance, and evolution is thanks to The Purple Crayon of Yale, Eric Berg, Frances Barney, the amazing Del Close, the Second City of Chicago, The Annoyance Theater, Upright Citizens Brigade (UCB), The Groundlings, Improv Olympic (iO), Magnet, and the too-numerous-to-remember thrown together troupes, late-night improv jams, and damn funny people I got to meet.

References

ABC News. 2005. "Study: Negative Words Dominate Language." February 2. http://abcnews.go.com/Technology/DyeHard/story?id=460987.

Anthony, S., D. Duncan, and P.M.A. Siren. 2014. "Build an Innovation Engine in 90 Days." *Harvard Business Review*, December.

Badal, S.B. 2014. "The Business Benefits of Gender Diversity." *Gallup Business Journal*, January 20. www.gallup.com/businessjournal/166220 /business-benefits-gender-diversity.aspx.

Bernstein, E. 2012. "Speaking Up Is Hard to Do: Researchers Explain Why." *Wall Street Journal*, February 7. www.wsj.com/articles/SB1000142405 2970204136404577207020525853492.

Bloom, T. 2015. "The 3 Most Innovative Sports Tech Products from CES 2015." SportTechie, January 8. www.sporttechie.com/2015/01/08 /the-3-most-innovative-sports-tech-products-from-ces-2015.

Bobkoff, D. 2014. "Bjarke Ingels: An Architect for a Moment or an Era?" NPR *Morning Edition*, January 3. www.npr.org/2014/01/03/259117207 /bjarke-ingels-an-architect-for-a-moment-or-an-era.

Bronson, P., and A. Merryman. 2010. "The Creativity Crisis." *Newsweek*, July 10. www.newsweek.com/creativity-crisis-74665.

Brown, S. 2009. *Play: How It Shapes the Brain, Opens the Imagination, and Invigorates the Soul*. With C. Vaughan. New York: Penguin.

Chetty, R., and N. Hendren. 2015. *The Impacts of Neighborhoods on Intergenerational Mobility*. Executive Summary. April. www.equality -of-opportunity.org/images/nbhds_exec_summary.pdf.

Dean, J. 2011. "The Zeigarnik Effect." PsyBlog. www.spring.org.uk/2011/02 /the-zeigarnik-effect.php.

DeLuca, L.S. 2015. "Why This IBM Engineer Tells High School Girls That Straight A's Don't Matter." *Fortune*, August 29. http://fortune.com /2015/08/29/lisa-seacat-deluca-advice-for-female-engineers.

Dweck, C.S. 2006. *Mindset: The New Psychology of Success*. New York: Ballantine Books.

Emmons, G. 2007. "Encouraging Dissent in Decision-Making." *Harvard Business Review*, October 1.

Fairchhild, C. 2015. "Why So Few Women Are CEOs." *Fortune*, January 14.

Glassdoor. 2014. "What Job Seekers Really Think of Your Diversity Stats." November 17. www.glassdoor.com/employers/blog/diversity.

Govindarajan, V. 2012. "A Reverse-Innovation Playbook." *Harvard Business Review*, April. https://hbr.org/2012/04/a-reverse-innovation -playbook.

Grant, A. 2016a. "Can Slowing Down Help You Be More Creative?" NPR, TED *Radio Hour*, part 2. August 26. www.npr.org/programs/ted-radio -hour/490624293/slowing-down?showDate=2016-08-26.

Grant, A. 2016b. *Originals: How Non-Conformists Move the World*. New York: Viking.

Gray, D. 2005. "Stuck?" *Communication Nation*, October. http:// communicationnation.blogspot.com/2005/10/stuck.html.

Griggs, B., and E. Grinberg. 2015. "Hedy Lamarr Gets Inventive Salute From Google Doodle." CNN, November 9. www.cnn.com/2015/11/09 /entertainment/hedy-lamarr-google-doodle-feat.

Henry, Z. 2016. "The Real Joy Mangano on the Biggest Challenges of Building a $3 Billion Empire." Inc.com, January. www.inc.com/zoe-henry/joy -mangano-miracle-mop-beating-the-odds.html.

"History of General Anesthesia." Wikipedia. https://en.wikipedia.org/wiki /History_of_general_anesthesia.

Horgan, J. 2014. "Tripping in LSD's Birthplace: A Story for 'Bicycle Day.'" *Scientific American*, Cross-Check blog, April 19. https://blogs. scientificamerican.com/cross-check/tripping-in-lsds-birthplace-a -story-for-e2809cbicycle-daye2809d.

Hough, K. 1998. *Collaborative Brainstorm*. Columbus, OH: ImprovEdge.

Hough, K. 2008. The Yes! Deck. Columbus, OH: ImprovEdge.

Hough, K. 2011. "Creative Constraint: Why Tighter Boundaries Propel Greater Results." *Mashable*, March 2. mashable.com/2011/03/02/creative-constraint-business.

HowStuffWorks.com. 2013. "10 Accidental Inventions You Won't Believe." Stuff of Genius blog, October 22. www.geniusstuff.com/blogs/10-accidental-inventions10.htm.

Hudson, M. 2013. "Blindspot: Hidden Biases of Good People by Mahzarin R. Banaji and Anthony G. Greenwold." *Washington Post*, February 8. www.washingtonpost.com/opinions/blindspot-hidden-biases-of-good-people-by-mahzarin-r-banaji-and-anthony-g-greenwald/2013/02/08/4c42d6b8-6a1b-11e2-ada3-d86a4806d5ee_story.html.

Hunt, V., D. Layton, and S. Prince. 2015. "Why Diversity Matters." McKinsey & Company, January. www.mckinsey.com/business-functions/organization/our-insights/why-diversity-matters.

Israel, P. 1998. *Edison: A Life of Invention*. New York: Wiley.

Jacobs, S. 2015. "35 Innovators Under 35: A Software Engineer Makes a Habit of Going After Everyday Problems." MIT *Technology Review*. www.technologyreview.com/lists/innovators-under-35/2015/inventor/lisa-seacat-deluca.

Jacques, R. 2014. "9 Reasons to Take a Vacation ASAP, According to Science." *The Huffington Post*, August 28. www.huffingtonpost.com/2015/09/05/take-a-vacation_n_5701215.html.

"Joy Mangano." Wikipedia. https://en.wikipedia.org/wiki/Joy_Mangano.

Junco, R., and S.R. Cotten. 2012. "No A 4 U: The Relationship Between Multitasking and Academic Performance." *Computers & Education* 59(2): 505-514.

Lafley, A.G., and R. Charan. 2008. *The Game Changer: How You Can Drive Revenue and Profit Growth with Innovation*. New York: Random House.

Laubach, M. 2011. "A Comparative Perspective on Executive and Motivational Control by the Medial Prefrontal Cortex." Chapter 6 in *Neural Basis of Motivational and Cognitive Control*. Edited by R.B. Mars, J. Sallet, M.F.S. Rushworth, and N. Yeung. Cambridge: MIT Press.

Luk, J. 2015. "Most Innovative Sneakers of 2015." *High Snobiety*, December 23. www.highsnobiety.com/2015/12/23/most-innovative-sneakers-2015.

Martinez, A.R. 2010. "The Improvisational Brain." Seedmagazine.com, December 14. http://seedmagazine.com/content/article/the_improvisational_brain.

Morin, R. 2014. "This Warden Wants to make His Job Obsolete." *Vice*, May 30. www.vice.com/read/this-warden-wants-to-make-his-job-obsolete.

New Hampshire Department of Corrections. n.d. "Mission Statement." Concord, NH: New Hampshire Department of Corrections. www .nh.gov/nhdoc/aboutus.html.

"NeXT." Wikipedia. https://en.wikipedia.org/wiki/NeXT#Original_NeXT_team.

Nye, H. 2014. "Saving Newborns in Malawi With Bubble CPAP." RT for Decision Makers in Respiratory Care, April 10. www.rtmagazine .com/2014/04/saving-newborns-malawi-bubble-cpap.

Olsen, E.G. 2015. "How Corporate America Is Tackling Unconscious Bias." *Forbes*, January 15.

Ophir, E., C. Nass, and A.D. Wagner. 2009. "Cognitive Control in Media Multitaskers." *Proceedings of the National Academy of Sciences* 106(37): 15583-15587.

Palca, J. 2014. "Saving Babies' Lives Starts With Aquarium Pumps and Ingenuity." NPR *Weekend Edition Saturday*, January 3. www.npr.org /sections/health-shots/2014/01/03/259436844/saving-babies -lives-starts-with-aquarium-pumps-and-ingenuity.

Pentland, A. 2014. *Social Physics: How Good Ideas Spread–The Lessons From a New Science*. New York: Penguin.

Poetry Foundation. 2016. "Samuel Taylor Coleridge Biography." www .poetryfoundation.org/poems-and-poets/poets/detail/samuel -taylor-coleridge.

Porath, C., and C. Pearson. 2013. "The Price of Incivility." *Harvard Business Review*. January-February. https://hbr.org/2013/01/the-price-of -incivility.

Prather, J. n.d. *Civility and Respect in the Workplace*. Rose-Hulman Institute of Technology. www.rose-hulman.edu/media/1267954/Workplace -Civility.pdf.

Rae-Dupree, J. 2008. "For Innovators, There Is Brainpower in Numbers." *The New York Times*, December 5.

Reznikoff, R., G. Domino, C. Bridges, and M. Honeyman. 1973. "Creative Abilities in Identical and Fraternal Twins." *Behavior Genetics* 3(4): 365-377.

Richardson, A. 2013. "Boosting Creativity Through Constraints." *Harvard Business Review*, June. http://hbr.org/2013/06/boosting-creativity -through-co.

Rockwood, K. 2016. "Inside the New Way Stuff Gets Made." *Inc.*, March.
www.inc.com/magazine/201603/kate-rockwood/3d-printers
-robots-smart-glasses-sci-fi-manufacturing.html.

Rothman, J. 2014. "Big Data Come to the Office." *The New Yorker*, June 3.

Sarnat, M. 2011. "The Powerful Fours of Creative Thinking." JrImagination
Blog, November 11. www.jrimagination.com/blog/2011/11/11/the
-powerful-fours-of-creative-thinking.html.

Sawyer, K. 2007. *Group Genius: The Creative Power of Collaboration.* New
York: Basic Books.

Schultz, H. 1999. *Pour Your Heart Into It: How Starbucks Built a Company
One Cup at a Time.* New York: Hyperion.

Singh, K. 2016. "Why We Need Women's History Month, in One Brilliant
Comic." *The Huffington Post*, March 3. www.huffingtonpost.com
/entry/womens-history-month-comic_us_56d73b78e4b0bf0dab34403d.

Surowiecki, J. 2004. *The Wisdom of Crowds: Why the Many Are Smarter
Than the Few and How Collective Wisdom Shapes Business, Economies,
Societies and Nations.* New York: Doubleday, 2004.

Trex, E. 2013. "15 Companies That Originally Sold Something Else."
Mental_Floss, August 20. http://mentalfloss.com/article/22822/15
-companies-originally-sold-something-else.

White, J. 2014. "Benefits of Being Bilingual in Business." LinkedIn Pulse, May
22. www.linkedin.com/pulse/20140522204700-68335342-benefits
-of-being-bilingual-in-business.

Wilkins, M.M. 2015. "Why Executives Should Talk About Racial Bias at Work."
Harvard Business Review, April 20.

Woolf, S. 2015. "10 Diversity Hiring Statistics That Will Make You Think."
ClearCompany Blog, July 9. http://blog.clearcompany.com/10
-diversity-hiring-statistics-that-will-make-you-rethink-your-decisions.

Zack, D. 2015. *Singletasking: Get More Done One Thing at a Time.* San
Francisco: Berrett-Koehler.

About the Author

 **Karen Hough** is the founder and CEO of Improv-Edge. She has been using improvisation as a catalyst for business training and consulting for more than 17 years. A professional improviser and actor for 25 years, Karen has performed in more than 100 live productions with the Second City of Chicago, Metraform/Annoyance Theatre, the Organic Theatre, the Purple Crayon of Yale, and many others. Her TV and radio credits include CBS, Miller, Earthshare, Eli Lilly, and S.C. Johnson.

While working as a senior sales executive in the network engineering industry in New York and Chicago, Karen originated and expanded the sales and management efforts of three separate technology start-ups, launched partner programs, and assisted in East Coast and national expansions. She founded her company, ImprovEdge, with the goal to bring the skills of improvisation—the ability to think on your feet, arrive at solutions through the side door, and communicate in ways that bring people together—to businesses to drive innovation and success. In 2012, ImprovEdge won the silver International Stevie Award for Most Innovative Company of the Year.

Karen was recognized in 2016 as an Inspiring Woman by the WNBA's Indiana Fever, and was also a recipient of the Athena PowerLink Award for outstanding woman-owned business and named a semifinalist in TechColumbus' Innovation Awards 2011 for Outstanding Service.

Her book, *The Improvisation Edge: Secrets to Building Trust and Radical Collaboration at Work* (Berrett-Kohler, 2011), was a number 1 Amazon bestseller in category and an 800CEORead Top 25 Business Book. Her second book, *Be the Best Bad Presenter Ever: Break the Rules, Make Mistakes, and Win Them Over* (Berrett-Kohler, 2014), won the Benjamin Franklin Gold Award and has been translated into four languages. She is the creator/author of the Yes! Deck, Managing Tough Conversations: The Everyday Coaching Model. Karen is also a regular contributor to the Huffington Post and has been featured in *Inc* magazine, *Investor's Business Daily*, *TD* magazine, Mashable.com, and BusinessInsider.com.

A graduate of Yale University and La Sorbonne, Paris IV, Karen is a Certified Speaking Professional and an international conference keynote speaker on topics such as negotiation, women's issues, innovation, diversity, leadership, executive presence, managing tough conversations, and presentation skills.

Karen is deeply committed to volunteer activities and philanthropy. Her volunteer activities include teaching improv classes for high school students in rural Kansas and confidence-building workshops for children in Chicago's inner city. She resides in Columbus with her husband and three children.

Index

K

Kerr, Michelle, 48–49
King, Martin Luther Jr., 20–21
knowledge, as barrier to creativity, 43
"Kubla Khan" (Coleridge), 38

L

law firm case study, 9–10
lightbulb, teamwork and invention
of, 41
Lightwell case study, 48–49
listening. See focus, importance to
creativity
LSD, 60–61
luck, defined, 26
lulls, in brainstorming sessions, 19–22
LWOW (Law Without Walls), in
upside down case study, 67–70

M

Managing Tough Conversations
workshop, 83–85
Mangano, Joy, 46–47
Martinez, Amanda Rose, 39
McConnell, David H., 59
medical device company,
preparation case study, 26–30
Miracle Mop, 46–47
mistakes, embracing the unexpected
and, 2–3
Mitra, Sugata, 65–66
multitasking, as enemy of focus, 38–39

N

negativity
in communication, case study of
responses to, 9–10
as problem for innovation, xiii–xiv
New Hampshire Department of
Corrections, 56–58
nonexperts, value to teams, 42–44

O

observations, managing change and, 80
"oops" moment, embracing the
unexpected and, 2–3, 6

open-ended questions
brainstorming and, 28
managing change and, 80–81
Originals/outliers, 20, 64–65

P

pain management, innovation and, 60
Paliwal, Dinesh C., 7–8
Pass the Pen game, 59–60
Pearson, Christine, 57–58
Pentland, Alex, 77–78
personal connections, benefits of, 77–78
*Philosophical Transactions of the
Royal Society B*, 17
play, 35–50
commitment and, 44–48
focus and, 36–40
Lightwell case study, 48–49
story game exercise, 50
teamwork and, 40–42
value of, 35–36
value of nonexperts to, 42–44
*Play: How It Shapes the Brain, Opens
the Imagination, and Invigorates
the Soul* (Brown), 35–36
Porath, Christine, 57–58
positivity, innovation and, xi, xiv–xv,
6, 10, 68
power plant ski slope idea, 19
practice, preparation and, 26
PREcrastinators, 20
preparation, 15–31
brainstorming and, 16–22
collaborative brainstorming
exercise, 30–31
environment for creativity and,
23–26
medical device case study, 26–30
practice and, 26
procrastination, outliers and
innovation and, 20
psychedelic drug, innovation and, 60–61

Q

questions, asking when managing
change, 80–81

R

racial diversity, team performance and, 4
reflections, brainstorming and, 28–29
reverse-innovation, 7–9
Rice University, 43–44
Richardson, Adam, 62
ridiculous ideas, in brainstorming sessions, 18–19
Rock, David, 78

S

Saras (teams), 7–8
Sawyer, Keith, 41–42
Schwartz, Jeffrey, 78
Seed magazine, 39
Singletasking (Zack), 38
Social Physics (Pentland), 77–78
status quo, challenging of. *See* upside down thinking
story game exercise, 50
stress
    controlling with breathing, 79–80
    as enemy of focus, 39
    see also anxiety; discomfort
Surowiecki, James, 43
suspension of disbelief, play and, 44–45
Suzuki, Shunryu, 43

T

T.A.G. (acronym game) exercise, 70–71
teamwork, value of, 40–42
"telling," in improv game, 82
tension, creativity and innovation and, 1–8
"third ideas," 55
Time Dash game, 81–82
Tomlin, Lily, 61
Torrance, E. Paul, 5
trickle-up (reverse) innovation, 7–9
trust, managing change and, 78–80
Tushman, Michael, 75–76

U

Ultimate Challenge, 63–64
unexpected, embracing of, 1–11
    diversity and, 3–4

how we learn exercise, 10–11
law firm case study, 9–10
mistakes and, 2–3
tension and creativity, 1–8
up-front work. *See* preparation
upside down thinking, 55–71
    challenge to status quo and, 56–58
    computers in India as example of, 64–66
    creative constraints and, 61–64
    justification and, 58–61
    Law without Walls case study, 67–70
    T.A.G. exercise, 70–71

V

vacations, creativity and, 48
Van Wickler, Rick, 56–58
Virginia Tech study, 17

W

Watts, Alan W., 36
Wells, Horace, 60
WhiteHatters, 69
"Why not?" mantra, 49
Winfrey, Oprah, 47
Wisdom of Crowds, The (Surowiecki), 43
Wozniak, Steve, 41
Wrigley, William Jr., 60

Y

"Yes, and" principle
    brainstorming and, 18, 19, 28–29
    embracing the unexpected and, 1, 6, 8, 10
    innovation teams and, xv
    power of, xiii–xiv
    upside down thinking and, 68
Yes! Deck toolkit, x

Z

Zack, Devora, 38
Zeigarnik, Bluma, 21
Zuckerberg, Mark, 47